O9-AIF-532

# THE LIFE RECOVERY® WORKBOOK

**A Biblical Guide through the Twelve Steps**

## STEPHEN ARTERBURN and DAVID STOOP

with
Larry Werbil
and
Janelle Puff

Tyndale House Publishers, Inc.
Carol Stream, Illinois

Visit Tyndale online at www.tyndale.com.

TYNDALE, Tyndale's quill logo, and *Life Recovery* are registered trademarks of Tyndale House Publishers, Inc.

*The Life Recovery Workbook: A Biblical Guide through the Twelve Steps*

*The Big Book* is a registered trademark of A.A. World Services, Inc.

Copyright © 2007 by Stephen Arterburn and David Stoop. All rights reserved.

Cover photograph copyright © by Thinkstock. All rights reserved.

Cover design by Koechel Peterson & Associates.

Edited by Linda Schlafer

Published in association with the literary agency of Alive Communications, Inc., 7680 Goddard Street, Suite 200, Colorado Springs, CO 80920.

Unless otherwise indicated, all Scripture quotations are taken from the *Holy Bible,* New Living Translation, copyright © 1996, 2004, 2007 by Tyndale House Foundation. Used by permission of Tyndale House Publishers, Inc., Carol Stream, Illinois 60188. All rights reserved.

Scripture quotations marked NIV are taken from the Holy Bible, *New International Version,*® NIV.® Copyright © 1973, 1978, 1984 by Biblica, Inc.™ Used by permission of Zondervan. All rights reserved worldwide. www.zondervan.com.

The brief excerpt from *Alcoholics Anonymous* and the Twelve Steps are reprinted and adapted with permission of Alcoholics Anonymous World Services, Inc. Permission to reprint and adapt the Twelve Steps does not mean that AAWS has reviewed or approved the contents of this publication, or that AAWS necessarily agrees with the views expressed herein. A.A. is a program of recovery from alcoholism *only*—use of the Twelve Steps in connection with programs and activities which are patterned after A.A., but which address other problems, or in any other non-A.A. context, does not imply otherwise. Additionally, while A.A. is a spiritual program, A.A.is not a religious program. Thus, A.A. is not affiliated or allied with any sect, denomination, or specific religious belief.

The profiles in this workbook are composite characteristics of persons who have had the courage to work the steps on various issues in their lives and on their own addictive behaviors. Names, ages, and situations have been modified to protect their anonymity.

ISBN 978-1-4143-1328-3
ISBN 978-1-4143-1959-9 (BAC edition)

Printed in the United States of America

19  18  17  16  15  14  13
16  15  14  13  12  11  10

*This workbook is dedicated to every fellow struggler who has had the courage to face the truth about themselves, the humility to abandon their flawed attempts at living, and the willingness to find God's truth and live accordingly.*

# CONTENTS

## The Twelve Steps of Alcoholics Anonymous

1. We admitted we were powerless over alcohol—that our lives had become unmanageable.

2. Came to believe that a Power greater than ourselves could restore us to sanity.

3. Made a decision to turn our will and our lives over to the care of God *as we understood Him.*

4. Made a searching and fearless moral inventory of ourselves.

5. Admitted to God, to ourselves, and to another human being the exact nature of our wrongs.

6. Were entirely ready to have God remove all these defects of character.

7. Humbly asked Him to remove our shortcomings.

8. Made a list of all persons we had harmed, and became willing to make amends to them all.

9. Made direct amends to such people wherever possible, except when to do so would injure them or others.

10. Continued to take personal inventory and when we were wrong promptly admitted it.

11. Sought through prayer and meditation to improve our conscious contact with God, *as we understood Him*, praying only for knowledge of His will for us and the power to carry that out.

12. Having had a spiritual awakening as the result of these Steps, we tried to carry this message to alcoholics, and to practice these principles in all our affairs.

Copyright © A.A. World Services, Inc.

## The Twelve Steps

1. We admitted that we were powerless over our problems and that our lives had become unmanageable.

2. We came to believe that a Power greater than ourselves could restore us to sanity.

3. We made a decision to turn our wills and our lives over to the care of God.

4. We made a searching and fearless moral inventory of ourselves.

5. We admitted to God, to ourselves, and to another human being the exact nature of our wrongs.

6. We were entirely ready to have God remove these defects of character.

7. We humbly asked God to remove our shortcomings.

8. We made a list of all persons we had harmed and became willing to make amends to them all.

9. We made direct amends to such people wherever possible, except when to do so would injure them or others.

10. We continued to take personal inventory, and when we were wrong, promptly admitted it.

11. We sought through prayer and meditation to improve our conscious contact with God, praying only for knowledge of his will for us and the power to carry it out.

12. Having had a spiritual awakening as a result of these steps, we tried to carry this message to others, and to practice these principles in all our affairs.

The Twelve Steps used in *The Life Recovery Workbook* have been adapted with permission from the Twelve Steps of Alcoholics Anonymous.

## APPRECIATION

*We want to thank Larry Werbil and Janelle Puff for the hard work and rich wisdom they invested in this project. You two are dedicated partners in helping those who are ready to move beyond isolated attempts at helping themselves.*

*We also want to thank Misty Arterburn for her editorial and content contributions, and for her support in the writing process. You are a valued part of this work.*

*Also, we would like to acknowledge this life-changing truth: "Since Christ suffered physical pain, you must arm yourselves with the same attitude he had, and be ready to suffer, too. For if you have suffered physically for Christ, you have finished with sin" (1 Peter 4:1).*

*Steve and Dave*

# INTRODUCTION

*He has showed you, O man, what is good. And what does*
*the LORD require of you? To act justly and to love mercy*
*and to walk humbly with your God.* (Micah 6:8, NIV)

This workbook is about transformation: from death to
life, from addiction to recovery. It is about walking humbly,
righteously, and mercifully with God while accepting and doing
his will. In our compulsions and addictions, we have opposed
God's will by hurting ourselves, our bodies, and our loved ones.
We have been separated from God and from other people. The
Twelve Steps are a path to finding that humble walk that leads
us out of self-centeredness and closer to God's heart.

We will be examining the Twelve Steps individually to con-
sider the challenging spiritual lessons that allow us to live free
of bondage every day. Each step has a new task for us, but none
of the steps is meant to stand alone. For successful recovery,
they are meant to be worked in order. Each step prepares us for
the next one as we develop greater humility and openness to
God.

Although the path of recovery involves hard and sometimes
painful work, it is worth the effort. God will meet us on this
path as we become willing to take each step toward new life. As
we apply ourselves, we lose our old coping mechanism of exces-
sive consumption and experience spiritual growth. Honesty,
humility, and courage are components of the vital faith that
can allow us to face any circumstance, difficulty, or feeling with
grace and strength.

# STARTING AND LEADING A GROUP

Recovery is best experienced in the context of a group. Two or more willing people can form a powerful bond as they study and work these steps together. Instantly, your struggles, problems, and hang-ups become a blessing to the group. As you open up, everyone else will feel more free to share from their own lives.

Being the leader of a group is actually quite simple. You can find many books on how to lead a small group, but here's a simple and effective way to do it:

1. Find a location in your home, a church, workplace, or school, and obtain permission (if necessary) to form the group.
2. Put up a few flyers announcing the time and place, calling it a support group, recovery group, or Twelve Step group.
3. Show up early, arrange the chairs, make some coffee, and welcome people as they arrive.
4. Start when you say you will start by opening in prayer and by reading the Twelve Steps and the correlating Scriptures.
5. Ask if anyone would like to share for three or four minutes. Don't allow others to "fix" the speaker, and if he or she goes on too long, be sure to enforce the time limit.
6. Make sure everyone has a copy of the workbook. Ask them to study Step 1 for discussion at the next meeting.
7. End when you say you will end by reciting the Lord's Prayer.
8. Be sure that everyone knows where to get a workbook and a *Life Recovery Bible,* if they don't already have one.
9. E-mail me—Stephen Arterburn at sarterburn@newlife.com —and tell me how it's going.
10. Feel good that you are allowing God to use you.

Please remember that working the steps is an art, not a formula. Most often, it is an individualized process.

God be with you on this journey. We pray that you will find healing, serenity, and peace of mind.

## PROFILE

After seventeen years of partying and drinking, Barry
decided that the only way to handle life was to stay drunk.
For the past year, he had kept an iced case of beer in the trunk
of his car at all times. He couldn't understand why his wife
wanted a divorce, why his kids were distant and angry with
him, or why his life was always so chaotic and stressful. He had
made repeated attempts to control events, his wife's behavior,
his kids, and his job, but he always ended up in a crisis after
a heated, tumultuous argument that left him feeling bitter.
Drinking was the only way for him to de-stress and find compo-
sure.

One night, after Barry had been drinking all afternoon and
into the evening, his wife became fed up with his disappearing
into the bottle, and she contemptuously announced that she
was leaving him. Though the particulars of the fight were hazy
to him, Barry woke up the next day full of shame and fear. His
pain, loneliness, and aggravation became unbearable. Life with
alcohol didn't seem worth continuing, but he wasn't sure that
he was able to live without it. His previous attempts to quit had
left him restless, irritable, and disgruntled. With a beer in one
hand, he called the Alcoholics Anonymous hotline to look for
help. They told him that there was hope and recommended
that he attend meetings.

When Barry arrived at his first meeting, the chairman asked

for the topic to be Step One: *We admitted we were powerless over alcohol and that our lives had become unmanageable.* As members shared their experiences, Barry was stunned to identify with most of their stories. He began to recognize his powerlessness over alcohol, and that by continually using alcohol to seek relief, he had allowed his life to become unmanageable. He understood their stories of painful experiences while under the influence, and the resulting hopelessness. His other amazing discovery was that others in the room were not only sober, but content. Recovery seemed like a positive option, instead of the drudgery he had imagined.

Barry learned that powerlessness did not mean helplessness, and that he could take actions such as attending meetings, having a sponsor, reading recovery literature, and drawing close to God. As he took action on what he was able to do, he could admit his powerlessness over alcohol.

After he had been sober for a while and worked the subsequent steps, his overall life did improve. Barry learned that he was powerless over more than alcohol, and that the consequences of his years of drinking were not magically removed. The relationship with his wife fell apart because his drinking had caused her so much pain that the bond between them had been destroyed. His children continued to hold resentments toward him, and his relationships with them were compromised. However, to stay sober, Barry had to accept his powerlessness over their responses and to accept responsibility for his behaviors that had provoked them.

## STEP **ONE**

### *We admitted we were powerless over our problems and that our lives had become unmanageable.*

The recovery journey begins when we confront the very first word in Step One: *We.* This immediately challenges the loner/isolationist in us when we are in our addictions and dependent on people and substances. Although we would be more comfortable with the word *I* and would prefer to get better alone, only *we* can recover. The Twelve Step program guides us into community, where all involved are a part of each other's recovery. The Twelve Steps are worked and lived in a group; independence is deadly for any addict.

Actually, spiritual transformation for anyone begins in community. When Jesus began his ministry, he created a group. When we look at the church in the book of Acts, we find groups meeting in homes. Living in open and honest community appears to be necessary for spiritual growth—we have to accept help from others in order to recover from whatever addiction or codependency issues we have.

*We admitted we were powerless.* Admitting that something or someone has beaten us and is more powerful than our own will confronts our pride, so we keep on acting out in our dependency/addiction, trying to prove that we *can* control it. By attending meetings and listening to other people's stories, we become more open to the possibility of recovery. Our pride must be shattered, a little at a time, because we will not recover without an admission of powerlessness.

Our very human nature rebels at the idea of powerlessness, which signifies our inability to escape our life of dependency/ addiction on our own strength. We must let go of image seeking and pride and tell the truth about our demoralized condition. Step One contains a potent paradox: by telling the truth about our complete powerlessness over addiction, we receive the power of choice in return.

To jump into recovery waters with both feet, we must go even deeper. Not only must we admit and accept our powerlessness over our dependencies and addiction, but we must also concede that our lives are unmanageable. This strikes a second blow to our pride and self-sufficiency. When under the influence of addictive thinking, a person believes, "I can handle anything. I can fix this by myself, without anyone else having to be involved." We have wanted others to believe that we "have it all together" and are self-contained. We continue in the delusion that there *should* be something we can do on our own, especially to clean up our own lives.

However, addiction leads to inefficiency on our jobs, dissatisfaction in our relationships, and quite often, to a sense that life is not worth living. Our emotional pain underscores the reality of our inability to manage our lives. Our loner, pull-myself-up-by-the-bootstraps mentality must give way to joining the "we" of recovery. We have to be rid of the "just Jesus and me" belief system that leads to more isolation and shame. When we realize that even God is in community (Father, Son, and Holy Spirit), we become aware of the fact that human beings were created to be connected to others. The rebel within us must now get off the throne long enough to accept the need for help from both God and others. Then we will find that God is willing to meet us in our unmanageable lives.

The meditations for Step One include some examples from Scripture of people struggling with powerlessness. Naaman had position and power in the military that blinded him to his powerlessness (see 2 Kings 5:1-15). He began to demand things from life, thinking that he was special because of his position. We may do this as well, both at work and at home. We may have an inflated sense of importance because of our ministry. We may demand things from our families or coworkers based on *our way*. Like Naaman, we will find that this type of pride that resists input and direction from others leads to isolation. Only God can deal with this rebellion in our hearts. The consequences of addiction are sometimes the only way by which God can break through to us.

Sometimes we arrive at powerlessness and unmanageability by losing everything, as Job did. Being in recovery and trying to walk a spiritual path does not mean that we will be spared our share of snags and obstacles. In these times, recovery can appear to be hopeless and not worth the work. The rebel in us that wants control will counsel, "This is just too hard. Your troubles must mean that God doesn't like you." At this point, we need a group of people to continue pointing us to God no matter what happens. We need people who will nurture hope even in the most difficult places. As we hit bottom and face our powerlessness over all of life, we need encouragers. We need to be reminded of Jesus' saying that "if you try to hang on to your life, you will lose it. But if you give up your life for my sake, you will save it" (Luke 9:24). This is another way of describing powerlessness.

By exploring our powerlessness, we will have to confront and oppose negative ideas that tell us that being powerless means being a victim. By coming to the end of our own power, we develop enough humility to hear the voice of God and do his will.

The apostle Paul—before his conversion and transformation, when he was still known as Saul—could not explore powerlessness at all. He was intoxicated by the power he could wield, even if it placed him in opposition to God's plan for his life. Yet, God pursued Saul, despite his power-hungry, murderous state of mind, to call him to a new direction, a totally transformed purpose. So that he could stop persecuting the gospel and start preaching it, God made him totally blind and dependent on others to lead, feed, and shelter him. He had to accept powerlessness and unmanageability in order to be used by God in powerful and amazing ways.

We must also first accept our powerlessness and inability to manage before we can be freed from addiction and become a channel for God in ways we could never imagine. We are so schooled in the thought that we can do anything we put our minds to that it is almost impossible to envision the power of God in us, doing what we have not been able to do to this point. God in us, shining through human vessels, gives us the ability to recover, to accept powerlessness, and to accept unmanageability. We are then opened to a life powered by God rather than by our dependencies, our addictions, or our fallible selves.

When God's power lives in us, we can be pressed by troubles, perplexed by life, and haunted by our addictions/dependencies, and at the same time experience peace in trouble, hope in perplexing situations, and a lifting of the compulsion to act out. When we admit our powerlessness, God's power flows in to fill us and accomplish what we could never do on our own.

# QUESTIONS FOR STEP **ONE**

**No-Win Situations** *Genesis 16:1-15*

1. What feelings do I experience as I acknowledge people in my life who have power (such as supervisors, spouse, religious leaders, and sponsors)?

_____

_____

_____

_____

_____

2. What do I try to escape from? What do I feel trapped by?

_____

_____

_____

3. How do I escape my feelings, such as anger, boredom, fatigue, or loneliness?

_____

_____

_____

4. When things do not go my way, or when I am in a no-win situation, what is my reaction (with relationships, work, promotions, kids who question or rebel, traffic, drivers in front of me, people talking on cell phones in public places, financial difficulties, people who hurt or disappoint me, or God, who seems to be silent)?

_____

_____

_____

_____

5. If I could, how would I change my response?

_____

**Dangerous Self-Deception** *Judges 16:1-31*

1. What is the longest time I have been able to stop addictive behaviors or using addictive substances?

_____

2. What are some of the reasons I use for starting my behaviors or substance abuse again?

_____

3. What are the things I think I can control? How do I lie to myself, and about what?

_____

_____

4. What is so scary about telling the truth?

_____

5. As I explore powerlessness, what blind spots have I discovered?

_____

_____

6. What are the results of pride in my life?

_____

_____

_____

**A Humble Beginning** *2 Kings 5:1-15*

1. What is the difference between humiliation and humility in my life?

_____

_____

_____

2. How do I regard myself as being a little more important than other people?

_____

_____

_____

3. What makes me *think* I am in control of anything?

_____

_____

4. How do I try to influence or control God or his representatives?

_____

_____

5. When have I placed expectations on other people or God?

_____

_____

_____

6. When have my attitudes shown that I believe I know better than God?

_____

_____

7. Why is it difficult for me to follow another's instructions?

_____

_____

**Hope Amidst Suffering** *Job 6:2-13*

1. What kind of people do I hang around with and trust—people who criticize, or people who encourage truth?

_____

2. What emotions can I identify when I am at the bottom?

_____

3. What have I done in the past to deal with pain or sadness?

_____

_____

**Like Little Children** *Mark 10:13-16*

1. What happened in the past that still provokes fear in me today?

_____

_____

2. When do I feel the most cared for?

_____

3. What do I see in my life that reveals God's care for me?

_____

_____

**A Time to Choose**  *Acts 9:1-9*

1. When I continue to pursue my own agenda without asking God for direction, what happens in my life?

_____

2. Are there areas of my life in which God may have to use extreme measures before I will listen for direction? Which areas?

_____

3. What will it take for me to listen to God?

_____

**The Paradox of Powerlessness**  *2 Corinthians 4:7-10*

1. These are examples of when I have demonstrated acceptance of my own powerlessness and God's powerfulness:

_____

_____

2. How do I respond to trouble?

_____

_____

3. How do I respond to being perplexed?

_____

_____

4. What do I do when it seems that God or someone else has abandoned me?

_____

_____

_____

## PROFILE

Ally was always overweight as a child and teenager. Her weight was a very sore subject in her family, but food was her main comfort for anxiety and depression. She never felt as though she fit in with others, and her friends seemed to be untrustworthy and two-faced. Food became her comfort, companion, excitement, and recreation.

Over the years, her weight continued to climb until she was hopeless about the possibility of having a slim body. She would have fleeting periods of weight loss, but was never able to make a lasting difference. Years of self-hatred and feeling marginalized by life made her disbelieve that God *could* or *would* help her with her food and eating problems. She struggled for self-esteem and tried many self-help strategies for learning to like herself despite the extra pounds.

When she walked into Overeaters Anonymous, a Twelve Step group for compulsive eaters, she knew that she was powerless over food. Step One was obvious to her. But Step Two, *coming to believe that a greater Power could restore her to sanity,* was a huge roadblock. The challenge of Step Two was to gain enough faith to believe that God could accomplish what she could never do. As with all of us, Ally's faith had to grow as she opened her mind to the possibility that God could actually help her with her specific problem.

By talking to a sponsor and other people in the program,

she learned to simply believe that God's power was there and that he was really interested in her food issues. She began with hesitant faith to ask God to remove the insanity—the obsessive thoughts about food, the time spent bingeing, the negative thoughts about self, and the damaging effects on her body. Over time, her trust and belief in God grew as she learned to let go of food one day at a time, follow a food plan, and trust God to help her act sanely around food. The surrender of her dependency, as we all must learn, came by taking opposite action around food even when she didn't feel like it. By surrendering daily, Ally felt closer to God without the "food fog." She regained wholeness and sanity around food.

## STEP **TWO**

### *We came to believe that a Power greater than ourselves could restore us to sanity.*

As we have faced our powerlessness to stop the deadly progression of addiction in Step One, we have admitted our complete defeat. Because there is no hope available within ourselves (our sinful, human condition), Step Two describes the process by which we look outside ourselves to develop hope that there is a Power that *can* stop the addictive process.

This step begins with recognizing that addiction is a season of insanity. What usually begins innocently as seeking pleasure, relief, or comfort becomes, over time, a coping mechanism for avoiding reality and responsibility. The pain of dealing with the upsets, hardships, and disappointments of life can wear down our faith and confidence in God. Substances and addictive behaviors can be a way of managing our stress and our sense of being out of control. As time goes on, unfortunately, this coping mechanism turns against us. Instead of relief and comfort, we find more difficulties and troubles. We multiply our problems instead of solving them.

When we face the fact that we have been, in a sense, insane

to think that we could make life work by acting out in our addiction, we see that our belief in God and in his Son, Jesus, has been nullified. Our faith has been overthrown by our addictive thoughts and behaviors, and we are headed toward spiritual disaster. Surrendering the reins of our life is not easy. We have to face our arrogant thinking and realize that although we believe in God, we have not allowed him into our lives in a real and practical way. We have not fully understood how desperate we are for his restoration and healing. When we can honestly accept that we are not God, and that he must have more room in our lives than we have previously allowed, we will come closer to releasing our arrogance. We have been trying to bend life to *our* will and have not considered God's will at all.

In the meditations on this step, we look at scriptures that describe what happens when we try to live in our own power. First, we begin to think that God is unfair; we begin to question him and wonder if he is really with us, as Job did. Our "insanity" in this case is in having the arrogance to think that we could actually see the whole picture as God does, and know what is fair or unfair. *Coming to believe* for Job meant accepting that he was a finite human, and that God is omniscient.

We may become grandiose like Nebuchadnezzar and think that we have the right to declare how life should revolve around us, our needs, and our wishes. This king looked at his successes and began to claim the credit for himself. He lost the humility of remembering that God rules and gives power and success "to anyone he chooses" (Daniel 4:32). His grandiosity of thought and attitude was revealed by the dream that he had Daniel interpret. Daniel pleaded with him to turn from his sin of grandiose thinking, but his ego was hooked by the pride of accomplishment: "By my own mighty power, I have built this beautiful city as my royal residence to display my majestic splendor" (Daniel 4:30).

God did not allow Nebuchadnezzar to continue in that way; he was humbled by God with a season of insanity and grazed aimlessly with the cattle in the fields until he acknowledged

God's power and sovereignty. This king's grandiose thinking is similar to the grandiosity of addiction—we try to make life work by medicating, avoiding, or filling ourselves with more and more sex, food, relationships, or substances. What eventually happens is similar to what happened to Nebuchadnezzar: we end up wandering aimlessly, humiliated, and not accomplishing much. His season of insanity was like our season of addiction.

After his pointless drifting, this king came to his senses by looking up to heaven and realizing that life did not revolve around him, but around God. In the same way, to be relieved of addiction, we realize that our way of dealing with life has not worked. Our years of medicating our emotions with substances or compulsive behaviors have not brought the sense of comfort we were seeking. As we face the insanity of choosing to cope with life in these ways, we look up to heaven to find the all-powerful God.

Addiction is also a type of insanity in the way that it affects our internal world. Jesus came upon a man who was called Legion because he had so many demons living in him. Addiction is like that—we become consumed with demons of envy, jealousy, fear, and hate that drive us away from relationships and toward the tombs of isolation, bitterness, and hopelessness. We need Jesus to restore us to our right minds, put us back on our feet, and heal our hearts, as he did for this man.

If our addiction goes on for years, we can become outcasts from society, like the woman in the Gospels with the issue of blood. We are cut off from relationships and are unable to find acceptance from people. Isolation and loneliness are terribly painful, and they are not what God intended for us. It is essential for us to restore our relationships and connections with people if we are to emerge from our addictions and make a successful recovery. Our insanity must be healed by our reaching out for God as this woman did. She hesitantly and feebly sought Jesus in the crowd, thinking, "If I can just touch his robe, I will be healed." Reaching out to others is a tangible sign that we are reaching out for God's healing in our lives.

Once we can face and accept that we have been insane in these ways, we are closer to recognizing how desperately we need God's touch to restore us. *Coming to believe* in Step Two is a process of becoming aware of a greater reality than anything we can see with our eyes. God is willing at any moment to help us overcome our addictive behaviors and unmanageable emotions. By engaging in this process, we allow God to restore us to right thinking and to clear faith in his power. Then we can be free from the isolation, the grandiosity, and the tortured thoughts and feelings that accompany addiction.

# QUESTIONS FOR STEP **TWO**

**Persistent Seeking** *Job 14:1-6*

1. How has life seemed unfair to me in the areas of family?

_____

_____

Trauma/abuse?

_____

_____

Addiction?

_____

_____

2. What are my objections to trusting God fully with my addiction and my life?

_____

_____

3. What emotions and questions do I need to be honest with God about?

_____

_____

_____

_____

4. Am I willing to work through the pain and unfairness of my life in order to find God and be freed from addiction? What holds me back?

_____

_____

_____

_____

**Grandiose Thinking** *Daniel 4:19-33*

1. When in my addiction, in what ways did I display the belief that I was only accountable to myself?

_____

_____

_____

_____

2. How have I tried to have power over the events, outcomes, and people in my life?

_____

_____

_____

_____

3. In what ways did I show that I forgot that God is ultimately in control?

_____

_____

_____

4. How have I avoided acceptance of God's power over my life?

_____

_____

_____

**Internal Bondage** *Mark 5:1-13*

1. What self-destructive behaviors have I inflicted on myself due to addiction? List and describe them.

_____

_____

_____

_____

_____

_____

_____

2. How has my addiction kept me from living my own life while finding myself more comfortable in "caves" of isolation, anger/ rage, or silent judgment?

_____

_____

_____

3. Have I begun to drop my insanity of living alone and being trapped in addiction? Am I ready to have Jesus visit me in my "caves" and cleanse me? If so, write out a prayer to him here:

_____

_____

_____

## Healing Faith  *Luke 8:43-48*

1. How have I tried to control my problems in my own power?

_____

_____

_____

2. What were the results?

_____

_____

_____

3. Is there any other way that I would like to try to control and manage it?

_____

_____

_____

4. Am I ready to do my part, as this woman courageously did, by reaching out for recovery in faith that Jesus' power will be there? Write a statement of readiness to God.

_____

_____

_____

**Restoration** *Luke 15:11-24*

1. How have my compulsions and addictions led me to compromise my values, convictions, and principles?

_____

_____

_____

2. How have my compulsions and addictions dehumanized me and brought me shame?

_____

_____

_____

3. In light of how my addictions and dependencies have degraded me, am I now open to a deeper level of believing that the power and forgiveness of God will restore me to sanity?

_____

_____

_____

**Coming to Believe** *Romans 1:18-20*

1. How have my experiences shown me that my way of living is not a satisfying or productive way to live?

_____

_____

2. How have I seen God's power at work in other people's lives?

_____

_____

_____

3. What are the signs that I am on the path and in the process of being restored to sanity?

_____

_____

_____

**Hope in Faith** *Hebrews 11:1-10*

1. Am I becoming able to believe that God can help me to live sanely? How?

_____

_____

_____

2. Can I now believe that as I reach out for God's strength and surrender to him, God's nature is to be present and ready to help and support sane choices? Why or why not?

_____

_____

_____

The delusion of power is a deadly lie to live with. We try to convince ourselves that we have control, and that we have the power within us to change. Often, those around us fortify the delusion and hide the evidence of our powerlessness from us. Then, in a rare moment of clarity, we come to see that we have made no progress, possess no power, and know of no path to follow. The fortunate ones discover that, in thousands of remarkable ways, God has been reaching for us and revealing that he can help, that he can heal, that he can restore. Finally, hearing God's truth and believing it leads every struggler from a place of hopelessness to the possibility of new life.

## PROFILE

Jay couldn't understand why life was always so difficult! Someone was always on his case. If only his boss wouldn't be so demanding. If his wife would keep off his back about things, he'd be a lot happier. And his kids! Why wouldn't they listen? Why did they have to learn everything the hard way? Why wouldn't they take his advice?

Jay had a problem with constant anger. He was always upset and off balance about something that didn't fit the way he wanted things to go. Someone or something was always messing up his plans. He became furious when no one would listen to his plan, his advice, or his way, which of course were better than anyone else's because of his superior intelligence and vast experience.

Anger had become a way of life, a way to show power, a way to feel intensely without intimacy, and a way to shut people out. He needed the anger because he was unable to be vulnerable enough to let anyone know how insecure and inadequate he really felt. It worked for him! No one wanted much to do with him for very long. In time, the stress and loneliness of trying to manipulate and control the world left him feeling hopeless and depressed. He had to find another way.

Jay sought God's guidance through a trusted person and began a process of recovery. In learning to apply the Twelve Steps to his life, he came to accept his powerlessness over others, over events, and even over his anger. When he reached Step Three, he saw that the problem wasn't everyone else—it was his expectations, demands, and need to feel safe that drove him to try to control everything.

His challenge was to have enough faith that God cared about his job, his family, his needs, and his dreams to turn them over, as the step suggests. He had been a Christian, but could he truly let go and allow God to be on the throne even in his everyday events and relationships? Could he let God take them and let go of his anger? He was experiencing enough pain, loneliness, and despair that he was ready to release all of these burdens to God. He prayed that God would accept him even with his fear, anger, and pride, and help him to construct his life according to God's will. Jay gave up his own plans, expectations, and outcomes, since God's will and plans were more suitable. He let go of his own will by trusting that God cared for him. He asked that God would help him to transcend his troubles in order to bring him glory. Jay had completed Step Three.

After doing so, he saw that his life had a different motivation—to please God and do his will. It was not God's will to be angry at everyone or expect everyone to live up to his expectations. This meant that he could make plans, but the outcome was in God's hands. He learned to "suit up [for life], show up, and leave the results to God." The burden of manipulating every detail of his own and others' lives was lifted because he could now see that the outcome of others' lives was God's business, not his.

## STEP **THREE**

*We made a decision to turn our wills and our lives over to the care of God.*

In Step Three, we truly turn over our will, our way, and our entire life to God, addiction and all. Making this decision seems simple. After all, didn't we commit our lives to Christ? Why wouldn't we want to turn over a shameful addiction after all the painful consequences it has caused? But this is more than salvation, and more than asking God to take away our consequences. In Step Three, we intentionally release our hopes, dreams, choices, addiction, compulsions, and relationships, and give God control over all of it. This is a one-time commitment, and it is also the step that opens the door to a lifelong endeavor. We practice it with ever-increasing willingness and trust.

In approaching the decision directed by Step Three, we are challenged to trust God on a deeper level than ever before. Trusting God with *everything* in our lives may be difficult because of our experiences, from childhood to the present, in which people have repeatedly broken our trust. Life has trained us to be skeptical and wary, to take charge of situations because we don't trust anyone. We may have learned to make life work on our own power because no one around us could be trusted to protect, help, and nurture us. As a result, we can make the mistake of generalizing that lack of trust to God, thinking that he expects us to take care of ourselves, at least in some parts of our lives and issues. Confronting our lack of trust in God's care is critical to working the Twelve Steps in our lives from Step Four through Step Twelve. To have a successful recovery, we must learn to completely surrender ourselves and our will. As Jesus said, the one who loses his own life for Jesus' sake will find it.

Turning over our addictions and dependencies is definitely like losing our lives. This is our comfort, entertainment, relief, and reward, like a best friend who shares life with us. Letting go of it seems impossible, lonely, scary, and not a lot of fun. "And then to let go/turn over my will and *all* my life? I'll have no life left," we cry.

The obstacles of the spiritual realm, our self-will and grandiosity, have held us in the clutches of addiction. They have created the illusion that we are in control. The message and task of Step Three is to face the fact that our control is not real. We may have *thought* we had control, but God has the ultimate authority and power. When we accept this, then our dependence upon him for the solution to our addiction and any other life problem becomes clear.

Believing that he cares for us can also be difficult. We may have experienced tragedy, abuse, or other suffering that has caused us to lose faith in his care. From our past life experiences, we can draw erroneous conclusions about God and his character. We may try to win his favor by being good, or at least by *appearing* to be good. Shame about our behavior during our addictive acting-out may have us thinking that we are outside the grace of God, and that he is just waiting to punish us.

So how do we turn our will and our lives over to the care of a God we do not trust?

Our lives are in the balance, wavering between the painful chaos of addiction/dependencies and the offer of new life through recovery. To make this decision, we affirm that we are taking a stand so that we can live. As Moses said in Deuteronomy 30:19, we have a choice to make: life or death. In our case, will it be addiction or recovery? Are we choosing the path that leads to death or to life? Although the life of addiction screams at us to seek perpetual excitement—or perhaps it is numbness we seek—we have to believe that the life God has for us is infinitely better, richer, and more satisfying. We don't have to explain God or understand him; we just need to surrender our lives to him.

As we choose to draw close to God, God brings his reconciling love and redemptive purpose into our lives. In Step One, we admitted that we do not have power over addiction (or over anything in our lives). In Step Two, we acknowledged that God does have power to heal addiction and to work in our lives. Now in Step Three we decide to turn everything over, let go, and ask for help. These acts of humility allow God's Spirit to draw near to us. When our self-will is out of the way, God can work in our hearts. There may not be immediate results, but in turning it all over to God, we exchange our heavy burdens for the rest and peace that Jesus brings. The weariness of an addictive life can be exchanged for rest. We don't struggle or fight the addiction off. We let go by letting the fight be his; we let Jesus get in the boxing ring with our compulsive desires while we rest on the sidelines, free to do his will. Over time, the obsession is relieved. It's all in God's hands now.

As we choose to give our will, our thinking, our decisions, and our behavior "to the care of God," we rest in the belief that he cares for us. He is with us no matter what life throws at us. With his power and his presence, we are able to stop acting out in the circumstances of our addiction. We are becoming free from the bondage of life-stealing addiction.

The Third Step decision to allow God to take over our whole life is the foundation of subsequent actions we will take to work the remainder of the Twelve Steps.

# QUESTIONS FOR STEP **THREE**

**Trusting God** *Numbers 23:18-24*

1. What in my life has taught me *not* to trust God?

_____

_____

2. What have I done to cause others not to trust me?

_____

_____

3. What keeps me from surrendering to God?

_____

_____

**Free to Choose** *Deuteronomy 30:15-20*

1. What is it about my understanding of God that blocks me from deciding to turn my life and my will over to his care?

_____

_____

_____

_____

2. How does fear affect my choices?

_____

_____

_____

_____

**Giving Up Control** *Psalm 61:1-8*

1. Where did I get the illusion that I can control other people or my circumstances, job, or life?

_____

_____

_____

_____

2. What stops me from giving up *my* life, so that I can find the life *God* intends for me?

_____

_____

_____

_____

**Redeeming the Past** *Isaiah 54:4-8*

1. How do I hold God the Redeemer at arm's length? Why?

_____

_____

_____

2. What fears have the most power in my life?

_____

_____

3. How is shame connected to fear in me?

_____

_____

**Submission and Rest** *Matthew 11:27-30*

1. Why do I *think* that I am able to handle my addictions/dependencies on my own with no help from outside myself?

_____

_____

2. How ready am I to be taught?

_____

_____

_____

3. What characteristics interfere with my being taught by Jesus or another person?

_____

_____

_____

**Discovering God** *Acts 17:22-28*

1. How does my life reflect my image of God at any given moment?

_____

_____

2. How do I define the word *surrender?*

_____

3. What is the difference between "my will" and "my life"?

_____

_____

**Single-Minded Devotion** *James 4:7-10*

1. What does resistance look like in my life?

_____

_____

2. What do I have to face in myself when I draw close to God?

_____

3. How is addiction connected to my resistance to God's direction in my life?

_____

There comes a point at which we can either merely *have* faith, or make a bold move and really *live* our faith. When we live our faith, we no longer only talk about our beliefs but our lives reflect them: What we believe and say and do all line up. But this alignment only happens when we have enough faith to turn everything over to God—every compartment, every hidden secret, everything—and acknowledge, perhaps for the very first time, that God is the Higher Power in our lives.

## PROFILE

This step aroused fear and negativity in Alan's heart. In fact, he was so daunted that he thought it would be impossible to actually do a *"fearless* moral inventory," even if he did want to recover! First, with his image of God, he thought that the "searching" part was so that God could hunt him down and retaliate for all the wrongs and sins he had committed. He didn't want to look, because he knew he had been immoral and lived like a heathen for many years before becoming a Christian. His addiction was not exactly pristine, either, so he found many excuses for not doing this inventory, or for putting it off indefinitely.

But now, life wasn't working very well. Alan was trying to overcome some major "habitual sins" through the power of Christ, but despite all the knowledge he had about Scripture, memory verses, and going to church, he was still failing miserably. Something had to change; he was depressed most of the time, and he felt that God was far away. His verve and passion were not the same since his conversion. If Alan were to find more complete serenity and freedom from his addiction, he would have to undertake the painstaking effort of letting go of his past. He was assured by his sponsor and others that it was the way to peace and long-term recovery.

Alan's sponsor helped him to see that the inventory was like taking stock of the assets and liabilities in a business, which eased some of his fear. He began to see that his instincts had become unruly and were taking over his life: he had a great need for belonging, he had become possessive and jealous, he needed success, he was driven by competition and envy, he needed love and affection, and he believed that he deserved more than he had been given. Seeing how these out-of-bounds instincts were keeping him stuck spiritually helped him to detach from their control. Writing out the inventory gave him time to think about his behavior, assess his part, and look more deeply at what was motivating his actions. He also inventoried his positive traits and behaviors.

He had an emotional and spiritual release that was like letting go of a burden that had long been weighing him down. He was surprised at the effect, and he started to have a more realistic view of himself. He still saw defects and wrongdoings, but he was released from shame. It was the first tangible evidence of his willingness to submit to the direction of the Twelve Steps, and thus to God's will.

## STEP **FOUR**

### *We made a searching and fearless moral inventory of ourselves.*

To this point in the Twelve Steps, the work we have done is mostly on our thought processes, attitudes, and beliefs as we have emerged from denial about the seriousness of our problems and our complete inability to change them. We have admitted our powerlessness over our problems, come to believe that God can and will help us escape their effects, and have decided to let go and let God take over our lives. As important as this decision is, it must be followed by action. The remaining nine steps describe the actions we must take to break away from addiction and establish freedom and serenity.

Step Four is the first tangible evidence of internal changes that have been occurring in our hearts as the result of the steps. The first three steps have guided us into growth in humility, and we have trusted God at a deeper level, which is exceedingly important as we face the task of Step Four. It is a fearful and heart-breaking exercise to face the brokenness of our sinful human condition. Most people delay this work indefinitely, out of pride or fear, telling themselves that it is a pointless, painful exercise. They might think, *If we avoid practicing the addiction by using the first three steps, then why do we need to look deeper?*

Remember that addiction is threefold: physical, emotional/mental, and spiritual.

It is wonderful and amazing when an addict is able to stop using the addictive substances and behaviors. However, the condition of powerlessness is not just physical. A mental obsession and a pattern of thinking about self and the world traps and tricks the addict into starting up again, *even when he's sober!* Emotional tirades, intensity of relationships, or even boredom can lead the addicted one to seek relief in the substance or behavior of choice. Thus spiritually cut off from God, the addict trusts the addictive ritual instead of trusting God to help him handle whatever life throws at him.

Recovery is the process by which we find new ways of coping and dealing with life instead of using and avoiding. The only way to proceed in that process is to uncover our shame and allow God's light and life to flow in and heal us. We have made a beginning in the first three steps, and now through working Step Four, we find the roadblocks to lasting recovery.

What is an inventory? When a business takes an inventory, it takes stock of what supplies and merchandise are there. Making an inventory shows us what is necessary, what is surplus, what is useless, and what is a liability. Our lives are like a business, and as such, we must take stock of our abilities, qualities, and traits, both good and bad. We must examine our accomplishments and our limitations. In order to stay clean and sober, and develop spiritually and emotionally, we must face even our worst secrets.

At the root of all addiction is our sinful nature, and specifically, our selfishness. We want to be on the throne! We want to control the direction of our lives and quite often the lives of those around us. "If they would only do as I tell them . . ." "If they would only listen to my advice . . ." "If they would only use their heads . . ." Our resentments and insecurities grow as we find ourselves unable to have that complete control. If we look at the origin of our problem relationships and difficulties, we almost always find that the root is a decision *we have made* based on selfish motives. That decision and its resulting action cause us to offend, harm, or betray others, and to invite retaliation. If we are to live in freedom, we must face this fact of our human nature and take continual action to correct such behaviors and any wrongs we have committed.

The basic forms of selfishness in all of us are resentments, fear, pride, envy, dishonesty, greed, and moral or sexual misconduct [lust]. All of these will block God's Spirit and make it hard for us to know his will or feel his presence. As these blocks are identified, we can be freed from the burden of trying to look good. The goal is to become more real and honest with people who are in relationship with us.

To be "searching and fearless," we must look at ourselves morally, because God is just and moral. This is difficult when we have been consumed by addiction and mired in self-will. Fear must be put aside, and humility will grow a little as we are willing to document our flaws and misbehaviors. We examine the people, institutions, situations, and events of our lives that have caused us pain and resentment, and we assess our part in them. We do not excuse others of their wrongs, but we see our side of the street. For the first time, we take responsibility for how we have been resentful and fearful, judgmental and critical, negative and isolating. Usually these responses originate from perceived or real threats to our self-esteem, pride, ambition, material or emotional security, and relationships, both acceptable and hidden.

The good news about this work is that we gain an honest

picture of ourselves, possibly for the first time. If we weren't so miserable and desperate for a new life, we wouldn't be this gut-level honest. We begin to see patterns of behavior that have caused us trouble time and time again.

If fear is a huge pattern for us, we must turn this over to God. If resentment is our reaction to being hurt or snubbed, we must learn to pray for the person that hurts us. Any resentment, whether justified or unjustified, allows that person to control us, even if he or she has forgotten the incident! Obviously, there is less room for God in our lives if we are controlled by resentments and fears.

Letting go of resentments and fears by working the first three steps on them will banish our irritable, discontented attitudes. Serenity and peace of mind can flow into our lives. Internal changes will become more apparent to others.

After a thorough, searching, and fearless inventory, we can gain a clear understanding of how basing our lives on *self* has kept us from freely walking close to God. It becomes clear that we have anesthetized the emotional and mental pain of our lives with our addictive substances and behaviors, further cutting us off from him. This first inventory is the beginning of a lifelong practice of self-examination that leads us out of addiction and into relationship with God.

## QUESTIONS FOR STEP **FOUR**

### Coming out of Hiding  *Genesis 3:6-13*

1. When and in what ways have I led a "double life," looking good on the outside while full of shame about my addiction inside?

_____

_____

2. By hiding my problems with image management, how has my shame taken root and grown in my heart? Am I fearful to admit what is there?

_____

_____

3. Am I ready to deal with "the dirt," to wash the inside so I can live free? What holds me back?

_____

_____

## Facing the Sadness *Nehemiah 8:7-10*

1. What painful memories keep me from going forward in writing a Fourth Step inventory? Describe them:

_____

_____

_____

2. What have I been afraid of facing?

_____

_____

3. What role has shame from past mistakes played in keeping me from starting and completing an inventory?

_____

_____

4. Does pride tell me that I don't need an inventory? Have I told myself that others who are in more dire straits than I am are the ones that really need it?

_____

_____

**Confession** *Nehemiah 9:1-3*

1. What behaviors over my lifetime have been offensive to God?

_____

_____

_____

2. What destructive habits need to be identified and confessed to God?

_____

_____

_____

3. What blocks and resistances do I have to being honest with God about my wrongdoings?

_____

_____

_____

4. What consequences from past wrong choices am I living with today?

_____

_____

_____

**Family Influence** *Nehemiah 9:34-38*

1. Are there people in my family of origin whom I have blamed for my life situations and resulting addiction? If so, who?

_____

_____

2. What resentments do I carry toward them, even if unrelated to addiction?

_____

_____

_____

_____

3. What truly brought me into the bondage of addiction and dependency (what is my responsibility, my part in it)?

_____

_____

_____

_____

## Finger-Pointing *Matthew 7:1-5*

1. Is it easier to look at the faults and shortcomings of other people in my life, past and present (such as bosses, coworkers, classmates, church members, pastors), than to recognize my own?

_____

_____

_____

_____

2. What is the "log" in my eye, the blind spot that has caused me trouble and given rise to pride, finger-pointing, and eventually to addiction?

_____

_____

_____

_____

3. Where and when have I stepped on people's toes and invited retaliation? Have I been proud, blaming, or fearful?

_____

_____

_____

_____

**Constructive Sorrow** *2 Corinthians 7:8-11*

1. In what ways have I avoided facing my sorrow about how my addiction has impacted my life and the lives of others?

_____

_____

_____

_____

2. Am I willing to set aside time to grieve and to allow humility to grow in me? When? What is my commitment to myself, my growth, and my recovery?

_____

_____

_____

_____

3. Am I bent on self-condemnation? Am I now willing to let God's mercy go with me as I examine my faults and their impact on others?

_____

_____

_____

_____

**God's Mercy** *Revelation 20:11-15*

1. Taking a moral inventory of ourselves here on earth will help to prepare us for the life to come. Is anything standing in the way of my taking action, such as pride or fear?

_____

_____

_____

_____

_____

2. As I trust God in Step Three, am I able to let go of pride and fear in Step Four and allow his will to be expressed through me? If so, write out a prayer of trust and willingness to complete Step Four.

_____

_____

_____

_____

_____

3. Write down a list and description of resentments, fears, wrong-doings, and character flaws such as pride, jealousy, domination of others, self-centered needs/wants, etc. (Use extra paper if necessary.)

Fears:

_____

_____

_____

_____

_____

Resentments:

_____

_____

_____

Wrongdoings (i.e., what actions have I committed which oppose my own and God's morals and values?):

_____

_____

_____

_____

_____

Character Flaws (remember that honesty and humility are character *strengths* that we are building here, so be as thorough and honest as possible to move toward long-term recovery):

Where have I acted out of pride, vanity, or a sense of superiority?

_____

_____

_____

_____

Where and when have I tried to dominate others (e.g., at work, home, marriage)?

_____

_____

_____

_____

What makes me jealous, envious, or covetous (wealth, good fortune, successful kids, functional families, jobs, and/or positions of others)?

_____

_____

_____

Where and when have I demanded that my wants and/or needs come before those of others, especially those of my spouse, children, or coworkers?

_____

_____

_____

_____

4. After careful self-examination, am I more convinced than ever that I need a Savior every day, not just for salvation, but to walk in freedom from addiction and sin? If so, write out a prayer to God that expresses your complete dependence upon him for salvation and freedom:

_____

_____

_____

_____

In Psalm 119:29, the writer pleads with God: "Keep me from lying to myself." If we never stop to observe and take note of our patterns from the past, and our defective and deficient ways of coping in the present, we consign ourselves by default to another day of self-deception. The inventory, when compiled with honesty and diligence, is the beginning of facing the truth about our need to grow in character and maturity.

## PROFILE

After making a searching and fearless moral inventory, Alan dreaded sharing any of it with a sponsor or spiritual advisor. There were things on his list that were "take to the grave" secrets. He blew off his first appointment with his sponsor by just not showing up. He told himself that it was enough to write it all down, and that God already knew all about it, so why should he have to be open with another person? He was fearful of the response he would get. He was afraid his sponsor would condemn or shame him—and then tell everyone else about it. No one person knew all about him; Alan had never been that honest! In fact, when people started getting to know him, he moved or changed jobs.

Again, it took time for Alan to be persuaded that the process of talking over his wrongs, his character, and his heart would give him peace of mind. When he was finally able to share face-to-face, he experienced the miracle of being accepted for who he really was—defects, assets, and all! Instead of continuing to hide behind the wall he had built to protect himself, he became vulnerable through Step Five and experienced himself as being part of the human race. Taking this step was a huge milestone in humility and character building that moved him closer to freedom from his obsessions.

## STEP **FIVE**

*We admitted to God, to ourselves, and to another human being the exact nature of our wrongs.*

As Christians, we can recognize that Step Five comes from the ancient church discipline of confession. James 5:16 says, "Confess your sins to each other . . . so that you may be healed." We were not meant to keep secrets, even about our most shameful acts. God calls us to be connected, to bear one another's burdens, and to open the eyes of our hearts. Addiction is in opposition to God's design because it thrives on secrets, sneaking, and hiding drinks, hits, or partners. Our first reaction to "admitting to God, to ourselves, and to *another human being*" is defensiveness and fear. We may decide that since we can see our own faults through the Fourth Step inventory, and God knows it all anyway, we don't have to be vulnerable to another person.

Such pride and ego block our spiritual growth and keep us at a distance from God and others. Knowledge and understanding alone will never result in recovery. In isolation and protected space, recovery efforts are easily sabotaged, as we create and maintain plenty of room for destructive behaviors to continue. It is easy to keep the veil over our eyes and the eyes of others as we remain in the shadows of denial. Our pride and shame become more ingrained when we avoid facing up to our actions or claiming who we really are.

To work Step Five, we must reach another level of humility and willingness. To have God in all parts of our hearts and lives, we must be able to admit our exact wrongs honestly and openly. By sharing our story of poor choices, poor relationships, and poor reactions to life (i.e., sin), we get a clearer picture of the behaviors we have sown that have led to the harvest of addiction. By being exact and specific, we can no longer fool ourselves about how badly our addiction and its consequences have affected our lives and those of people around us. The rationalizing mind of an addict can very convincingly minimize our behaviors. This confessional step initiates a new direction in our lives as we begin living to please the Spirit and harvest everlasting life.

Remember that the steps are not only about victory over addictive behaviors. They are also about ridding ourselves of the blocks that keep us from being of service to God and others. James clearly says that healing comes from confessing our sins to others, not just from recognizing our shortcomings. In doing so, we cleanse our hearts of resentments, bitterness, fears, and judgments and make room for the truly useful and good things God has for us. Our character assets will be more readily apparent to others and more available to God.

Who should this person be to whom we will entrust our moral inventory? Who can we trust to be part of our healing process? Jesus has modeled for us the type of person we should seek. We need someone who is more interested in our spiritual wholeness and our freedom and progress in recovery than in our individual transgressions. This person must be able to lead us through the shame and the fear while assuring us that getting unstuck is worth the risk of being fully known. Ideally, we can find someone who has been through the Twelve Steps personally, and who can listen with compassion and acceptance, not judgment.

As we read our Step Four "to another human being" in Step Five, our confidante helps us to look even deeper into "the exact nature of our wrongs." In Scripture, we find examples of public confession of sin or wrongdoing that have helped to break down denial of our very human difficulties. By admitting and examining the specifics of our sin as we work Step Five, we find a pathway to the deeper core problems that lead us to wrongdoing. As we come to know the truth about ourselves, "the truth will set [us] free" (John 8:32). A wall that has stood between ourselves, others, and God will come down. We can face our past, mired in addiction, pain, and shame, with a new attitude. A sense of humility and gratitude begins to form. We find that God does not give up on us, and that his compassion is unending. Step Five moves us forward toward freedom.

When we have completed this step, we may have a mixture of feelings, from relief to gratitude to confusion. We have now inventoried and disclosed our deepest moral and spiritual secrets. We have faced some difficult aspects of ourselves that we have wanted to deny before. Adhering to this process is a surrender in itself.

Now we must accept forgiveness from God and our confidante. It is not always easy to simply accept forgiveness—not avoiding or refusing, but just receiving. As we do so, we begin to see ourselves in better perspective as being neither better nor worse than others. We are just human beings trying to grow up and get along in the world.

This pathway to freedom, though tedious at times, brings great rewards. Instead of being more self-focused, we become less selfish. Instead of becoming more concerned about our image, we can be more real with others. Instead of being self-destructive, we have a newfound self-respect. Working this step to the best of our ability builds humility and freedom, which continue to grow throughout the entire Twelve Steps.

# QUESTIONS FOR STEP **FIVE**

**Overcoming Denial** *Genesis 38:1-30*

1. What am I avoiding in Step Four by delaying Step Five?

_____

_____

_____

2. What is the *exact nature* of my wrongs as listed in Step Four?

_____

_____

3. What interferes with my being honest about myself?

_____

_____

**Unending Love** *Hosea 11:8-11*

1. How do I react/respond to the truth that God does not give up on me?

_____

_____

2. What keeps me from being truthful with God?

_____

_____

3. What makes me think that I can hide anything from God?

_____

_____

**The Plumb Line** *Amos 7:7-8*

1. Have my morals and values been in line with God's? Explain:

_____

_____

2. Have I had morals and values without being able to apply them to my life? Explain:

_____

_____

3. What has kept me from staying in line with God's and my own morals and values?

_____

_____

_____

4. Am I ready to surrender to God's moral "plumb line" and share my Step Four Inventory? If not, why am I hesitating?

_____

_____

**Feelings of Shame** *John 8:3-11*

1. What scares me about sharing "the exact nature of [my] wrongs" with another human being?

_____

_____

2. Who is my fear related to in my past? How did this fear develop?

_____

_____

_____

3. Has there ever been a time in my life when I felt the fear and took action anyway?

_____

_____

4. Have I set the appointment for completing Step Five by sharing my Step Four Inventory? My commitment to myself:

Date:                Time:

_____

**Receiving Forgiveness** *Matthew 5:23-24*

1. Why would God want reconciliation before praise when we bring gifts to him?

_____

2. Does anyone have anything against you that needs to be reconciled? Who and why?

_____

_____

3. What would be the impact on your life if you opened yourself up to forgiveness of others and from others?

_____

_____

_____

**Freedom through Confession** *James 5:16*

1. Lack of confession and openness with others results in a self-constructed prison. Do you know what that is like? Describe it here.

_____

_____

2. How can confession result in such profound healing?

_____

_____

3. Reflect here on God's command to be open not just to him but also with each other.

_____

_____

_____

_____

**Escaping Self-Deception** *Lamentations 3:40*

1. As you examine yourself, can you admit to some self-deception in the past?

_____

_____

2. Does anyone have the freedom to speak truth into your life on a regular basis? Who?

_____

3. Ask three or four trusted friends to write five words describing your strengths and five words describing your weaknesses. Record them here and examine them to discover areas you can work on within your small group of trusted fellow strugglers.

_____

_____

_____

_____

## PROFILE

Sarah, a middle-aged wife and mother, was having arguments with her husband over money. Her frustration and intensity were growing worse. As her emotional disturbance grew worse, her advisor reminded her to work the Twelve Steps on this before she was totally out of control. After recognizing that she was powerless over her husband's behavior, she was able to turn him over to God. By examining herself in Step Four, she found she had been critical of her husband, she had shamed him and tried to control him, and she had been anxious and fearful. She shared her journaling with a trusted sponsor/advisor who directed her to Step Six.

In these steps, she looked at what these defects had done to her and to her relationship. Were they helping her to accomplish anything? If she had had enough of these defects and their consequences in her life, was she now ready to have God remove them? She had to face her fear of what might happen if God really did take these from her.

By journaling along these lines, Sarah discovered that she was really being driven by fear of the future, fear of looking bad financially, and fear of scarcity. These fears led her to control and criticize, and her pride and anger made her feel powerful. She was reluctant to give up that power because it meant that she might feel vulnerable. Trusting God with the finances seemed impossible.

When she could see that these defects of character (pride, fear, anger) were detrimental to her marriage, to herself, and to her relationship with God, Sarah was ready to have them removed, as Step Six suggests.

We must all discover, as Sarah did, that readiness to give up our defects occurs when the pain of acting them out becomes greater than what they do for us. Sarah had to learn that God would have to remove these defects because they were so automatic. Power to change her attitudes and reactions was just as nonexistent for her as for any other person struggling with an addiction or dependency. The humility to admit this is difficult to find, but when the pain outweighs the gain, we realize once again that God is the one who is all-powerful. When Sarah was ready to have God remove these defects, she could proceed to Step Seven.

## STEP **SIX**

*We became entirely ready to have God remove these defects of character.*

Step Six is a "pause" step. Here we reflect on the information we have received about ourselves in completing Steps Four and Five, by making an inventory of ourselves and admitting our faults and shortcomings out loud to another person. We have come a long way in developing a more accurate view of ourselves, in building deeper trust in God, and in recognizing the impact of our addictions and dependencies on ourselves and those around us.

Our work is not done, however. Inventory is just the first half of the process through which, if we are thorough, we will walk away free from debilitating addiction.

Now we must begin to allow God's Spirit to work deeply in our hearts, routing out our defects of character and making changes in our behavior and attitude that will bring wholeness and serenity.

At first glance, it seems obvious that we would, of course, be ready to have our defects of character removed. Why wouldn't we want to be flawless and blameless? Isn't it our goal in the Christian walk to be perfected in the image of Christ?

Some of our character defects have been useful to us, however, and they have sometimes been necessary for survival. It can be very difficult to let them go when they have been so automatic and so deeply ingrained, but to have a successful, serene recovery, we must let God chisel away even the defects that have been our default mode. This process of becoming "entirely ready" can bring grief—it's like letting go of old friends, and this is painful even when these defects have outlived their usefulness to us and to God. It is important that we take time again to reflect and even grieve about how the disease of addiction has affected us. We may have lost significant time with family and friends because of some of our character defects, not to mention our jobs and reputation.

Facing the brokenness of our sinful human condition is heart-breaking, as David learned in his life. He began as a "man after God's own heart" with enough faith to slay giants, but later in his life, he committed adultery and murder. His success in bold acts of faith as a young man led him to believe that he was invincible, or perhaps, after he became king, that laws and rules did not apply to him. Addiction is like that—it can embolden us to act profitably in the beginning, yet it brings grandiosity and arrogance, which lead to our rationalizing the breaking of morals, laws, and rules. As David faced the reality of his sin, he began to see the arrogance of his youth and the value of humility. Such humility before God is forged through "a broken spirit and a contrite heart."

One huge character defect for all of us is trying to make life work in our own power. As God says through the prophet Isaiah, "[You] spend your money on food that does not give you strength" (Isaiah 55:2). We often believe, in our self-sufficiency, that if we can only fill this hungry hole in our souls with alcohol, food, sex, money, power, or pornography, we will be satisfied. These turn out to be empty wells, but we keep compulsively running to them. We become addicted and dependent.

In Step Six, we become *entirely ready* by once more acknowledging that our ways of handling life, even if they have helped us survive in the past, are not what God intends for us. We become ready to have God remove these defects, while acknowledging that we have no power to change ourselves. Here again, we must have our prideful ego dashed if we are to have freedom and serenity. If, after looking at our list of defects, we embark on our own self-improvement program, we may pour a lot of frantic energy into "getting better" and "trying harder" without any real change occurring. The removal of defects is a spiritual surgery that must be accomplished by God's hand. We must let go of the struggle, give over our will on each defect of character, and become open to his work in our heart. Grasping our complete dependence upon him for lasting change takes a great deal of humility and willingness.

However, let us not assume that we are to sit around and wait for God to work magic on us. *Becoming ready for him to remove our defects* means that we develop humility and willingness, and become open to behaving and acting differently. The interaction between Jesus and the crippled man lying by the pool of Bethesda exemplifies this aspect of Step Six. Like this man, we who are addicted have a sincere desire to be healed, to rise up and be productive, and to live a meaningful, purposeful life. We may get ourselves right to the edge of significant progress in recovery, but our character defects have crippled us so that we are paralyzed by fear and cannot get to the next level. We have to let go of familiar patterns that are easy for us even if they are hurtful or debilitating. We may be daunted by the prospect of living in reality with no anesthetic (our addictive behaviors). It's too risky! Fear of failure, rejection, or abandonment set in, and we sit by the side of the pool, complaining about our helplessness or feeling sorry for ourselves because we must change and work at sobriety when the rest of the world can still enjoy the pleasures of whatever addiction is our comfort.

This step focuses our attention on "being entirely ready," as though Jesus were saying to us: *Would you like to get well?* As we look inside our hearts, all our excuses, resistance, procrastination, and avoidance of recovery pop up, as for this crippled man. Jesus doesn't validate our excuses. He challenged the man to get up, pick up his mat, and walk. Jesus is challenging us in this step "to have God remove all these defects of character." In other words, we are invited to step out in faith, take action toward the recovery behaviors we need to develop, and leave the rest to God. When this man took action, God's healing took place. When we do our part by choosing to act differently in the moment, God removes the defects!

No matter how scary or uncomfortable it may be, we can become willing to take new actions toward fulfilling God's will. We may not *feel* like being honest where we have been dishonest. We may not *feel* like being considerate when we have been selfish. We may not *feel* like courageously facing our problems head-on instead of running from responsibility. But when we *become entirely ready,* we are *willing* to allow God to help us to be and to do what we have been unable to do on our own. When we willingly do our part by living rightly in the moment, God removes our defects by supplying his power and his Spirit to make these changes in us. Over time, our defects are replaced with character strengths.

Working Step Six in this way prepares us for Step Seven.

# QUESTIONS FOR STEP **SIX**

**Taking Time to Grieve** *Genesis 23:1-4; 35:19-21*

1. What are the defects identified in Steps Four and Five that are standing in the way of my recovery and service to God? Make a list.

_____

_____

What have each of these defects done *for* me and *against* me?

| Defect | Positive | Negative |
|--------|----------|----------|
| _____ | _____ | _____ |
| _____ | _____ | _____ |
| _____ | _____ | _____ |
| _____ | _____ | _____ |
| _____ | _____ | _____ |
| _____ | _____ | _____ |

As you look at this list, take some time to grieve. Feel the pain of the losses of both the positive and the negative parts. Some suggestions:

- Write about what you will miss about your defects and what you look forward to when these are removed.
- Write what you have learned about yourself in seeing the positive and the negative parts.
- Have a "burial" service. The old has passed away, so burn what you have written, or rip up the list of defects.

**Healing the Brokenness** *Psalm 51:16-19*

1. How have the last five steps prepared me to be "entirely ready" for God to work in my heart?

_____

_____

_____

_____

2. In this psalm, David had to grow up a little. He had to accept that he was flawed in God's eyes, and that he could never bring a sacrifice good or perfect enough to atone for those flaws. Am I still trying to bring God evidence of how good I am, or am I

coming to a place of acceptance, as David did? How does that acceptance help me stay out of my addiction? Explain:

_____

_____

_____

_____

## God's Abundant Pardon *Isaiah 55:1-9*

1. In what ways have I tried to fill the hunger of my soul and the thirst of my spirit with other substances and behaviors instead of trusting and following God's will?

_____

_____

_____

_____

2. Am I ready to turn to God for abundant pardon and for continual nourishment of his Spirit to keep me free of addictive behaviors? Why or why not?

_____

_____

_____

_____

3. Do I believe, not just in my head, that the life God has for me will be more satisfying than the one I have lived under the cloud of addiction? Is my heart willing?

_____

_____

_____

**Removing Deeper Hurts** *Jonah 4:4-8*

1. What deeper problems did my addiction shelter from my aware-
ness? Pride? Egocentrism? Fear? Anger? Hatred? The arrogance
of believing that life should go the way I want?

_____

_____

_____

_____

2. What difficulties have I suffered due to lack of forgiveness or
compassion for others?

_____

_____

_____

_____

3. Am I ready to have these defects removed by God? Why or why
not?

_____

_____

_____

_____

**Discovering Hope** *John 5:1-15*

When we are ready, God does his part. Our part is to get rid of
excuses, stubborn resistance, holding on to the familiar, and fear
of change. When we clear out these blocks and become entirely
ready, it becomes clear that God must do the rest, because only he
can accomplish the miracle of setting our feet on the path of life
again.

1. What have been my excuses for not moving forward in recovery?

_____

_____

_____

_____

_____

2. Have I been stubbornly resistant to becoming entirely ready because I have been afraid of change? Are my defects too comfortable and familiar?

_____

_____

_____

**Removed, Not Improved**  *Romans 6:5-11*

1. What self-improvement tactics and methods have I used to get myself to let go of my addiction and character flaws?

_____

_____

_____

_____

2. Meditate and dwell on the thought that "we are no longer slaves to sin [addictions]. For when we died with Christ we were set free from the power of sin [addictions]" (Romans 6:6-7). Describe the feelings that arise during that time of reflection.

_____

_____

_____

_____

**Attitudes and Actions** *Philippians 3:12-14*

This is the attitude of Step Six: "I don't mean to say that I have already achieved these things or that I have already reached perfection. But I press on to possess that perfection for which Christ Jesus first possessed me" (Philippians 3:12).

1. Do I have a vision of the purposes for which God saved me spiritually and took me out of addiction? Describe:

_____

_____

_____

_____

2. Am I now willing to accept that I will continue taking this step in order to grow, letting go of the old flaws to make room for the new strengths? Why or why not?

_____

_____

_____

_____

To be ready to battle means that we are appropriately equipped to meet the enemy. When we are ready to allow God to clean things up, there are battles to be fought that require us to be armed and ready. First Peter 4:1 seems to hold the key to what prepares us for battle with our character and its defects.

Peter tells us to arm ourselves with the attitude of Christ, who was prepared and willing to suffer. For it is when we are willing to suffer that we are ready to stop sinning. Are you ready? If not, it's time to become ready.

# PROFILE

Sarah was recognizing that her automatic responses of criticism, anger, and explosions resulted from her trying to make life work on her own power in the areas of her marriage and finances. It became obvious that her will was unproductive when she assessed the damage and the difficulties that her way was causing. She had to become ready for the defects to be removed if she wanted to have peace and a growing relationship.

To work Step Seven, Sarah focused on the humility to do God's will in her relationship with her husband and around her finances. She prayed to have the defects of fear, anger, criticism, and pride removed, as much as God would for that day, especially when she was dealing with her husband. Her responsibility was to take opposite actions when she was tempted to lash out or have a proud attitude. She wrote out her prayer to be able to offer kindness, respect, and positive, direct communication with him. In doing so, she conformed her will to God's will. This allowed Sarah to work as a team with her husband to improve their financial situation, and the entire relationship became more positive.

As she worked on this step daily by asking God to remove these defects, Sarah was practicing the principle of humility. This prepared her spirit to allow God's strengths to fill those places where the defects had been. Over time, her tirades and resentment toward her husband diminished, she could be more calm and rational when communicating with him, and they could build trust again.

## STEP **SEVEN**

### *We humbly asked God to remove our shortcomings.*

After we have become ready for God to work on removing our character defects, the Seventh Step is fairly easy: asking him to do his work. When we have truly worked Step Six, we clearly see that our defects have been holding us back from being a channel for God's Spirit. From a sincere desire to be changed inside out, we humbly ask him to remove our shortcomings and build our character.

This is a turning point in our recovery. While we have been focused earlier on stopping the progression of our deadly addictions and compulsions, we must now also let go of the *spiritually* deadly traits that have kept us from being who we really are. We begin to allow God's Spirit to flow into our lives and replace character defects with character strengths. We get out of our own way, accepting that our way of dealing with life has been problematic for us, others, and God. This is part of the development of humility.

Some of us confuse humility with humiliation. We have been through a lot of humiliating experiences because of our addiction. We have been humiliated by the consequences of addiction, such as jails or broken relationships. We have been humiliated in childhood. Most of us want to avoid being humiliated at all costs, so when the word *humility* is used here, many will not want to have anything to do with it. We have not understood that humility is a quality of spirit that opens the door of our hearts to God. It has nothing to do with humiliation and shame. Humility is an attitude in which we see ourselves in totality, the good and bad parts, the honesty and dishonesty, self-centeredness and selflessness—in other words, as neither the best nor the worst, just as a human. Humility is not a sign of weakness; admitting the negative as well as the positive is a sign of authenticity. We become real with God and ourselves.

We may be confused because we have believed in God and had strong religious convictions, yet we have not been able to stop using substances, people, food, or sex. Our Bible studies and prayer meetings have not helped us to curb our angry outbursts at home, our controlling attitudes at work, or our problem with anxiety and fears. This is usually because we have tried to play God, relying on self-will and self-propulsion. Somehow, we think that *we* must take charge of our recovery, direct our progress, and push for changes. We may even try to whiz through the rest of the steps as if recovery were a race. Our plans, our strategies, and the tactics on which we have depended to get us through life have been nothing more than self-will. We became focused on what we wanted and when we wanted it. Despite our convictions and beliefs, pride and ego edged God out!

Consequently, Step Seven challenges us to embark on the development of our spirits, to let go of directing and managing our image, and to throw ourselves on the potter's wheel to be molded and shaped by his hand, as described in Jeremiah 18. In Isaiah 45:9, an ominous warning comes to Isaiah from God. "What sorrow awaits those who argue with their Creator." If we do not allow God to mold and change us, but still cling to some addictive behaviors such as self-righteous anger or controlling rage, our addiction will eventually return. We must grow and allow God to shape our internal character, or relapse is inevitable.

The awe-inspiring news is that God has a great desire to free us from addictive behaviors and to clean up the resulting character defects:

> *I restore the crushed spirit of the humble and revive the cour-*
> *age of those with repentant hearts. . . . I have seen what they*
> *do, but I will heal them anyway!* (Isaiah 57:15, 18)

The only prerequisite is the contrite and humble spirit for
which the first six steps have been preparing us.

As we have assessed the damaging effects of addiction on
our lives and the lives of others, our desire to be cleansed and
molded has intensified. We have found that sobriety in itself is
a good goal, but to have serenity, solid integrity, and self-respect
as well, we must have a change of heart and behavior. With this
step, we simply and humbly ask for the removal of our defects
and prepare to act differently.

Our first taste of humility was when we admitted our powerlessness over our addiction. Usually, our admission has been the
result of repeated problems and humiliations. Now we see that
this is just the beginning of a lifelong process in which God
brings us closer to his image and purpose.

God will not hammer down the door of our hearts. "Look! I
stand at the door and knock," Jesus says in Revelation 3:20. "If
you hear my voice and open the door, I will come in, and we
will share a meal together as friends." We must open the door
by reaching for humility and earnestly seeking to do his will,
knowing that depending on our own individual strength is useless. After becoming ready for God to come in (Step Six) and
then asking to have our shortcomings removed (Step Seven), we
must do our part in the character-building process by putting
positive new traits into action. We begin to practice new ways
of thinking, behaving, and treating people. Where we have
been dishonest, we act honestly. Where we have been selfish,
we act with consideration and selflessness. Where we have hidden from responsibility, we face it with courage. Where we have
run from conflict, we seek to resolve it peacefully.

When we begin to practice new behaviors, they will feel
forced and unnatural, as if we were learning a new dance step

with two left feet. If we are intentional and consistent over time, we will be gratified to find that our authentic personality is emerging. As a freshly cleaned cup can hold refreshing water, we are open to God's filling of our spirit. Freedom from addiction will become more automatic, and we will have clearer self-respect as we draw closer to God and to others.

# QUESTIONS FOR STEP **SEVEN**

### Clearing the Mess *Isaiah 57:12-19*

1. Have I developed enough humility from my experiences in addiction to see that I need to let God work in my heart? Is there any doubt that self-reliance has kept God out?

_____

_____

_____

_____

2. Describe the difference between humiliation and humility:

_____

_____

_____

### Giving Up Control *Jeremiah 18:1-6*

1. Have I ever demanded to have circumstances changed for my benefit? When?

_____

_____

2. Have I ever become impatient with God's timing in the process of changing my heart and character?

_____

_____

_____

_____

3. What keeps me from letting go so that God can shape my life better than I could ever imagine or create myself?

_____

_____

_____

## Pride Born of Hurt  *Luke 11:5-13*

1. Is it hard for me to ask anyone, even God, for help? What keeps me from sharing?

_____

_____

_____

2. What experiences in my family of origin have brought about this self-sufficiency?

_____

_____

_____

3. Have I held back from asking God for what I need because I am projecting my disappointments onto him? Do I trust him?

_____

_____

4. Am I willing to give up self-sufficiency and pride to persistently ask for God's help in removing my shortcomings?

_____

_____

_____

_____

## A Humble Heart  *Luke 18:10-14*

1. Have I ever compared my faults, problems, and sins to blatant sins of others such as robbery, murder, and adultery to justify avoiding deeper work on my own character defects? What does this do for me?

_____

_____

_____

_____

2. Have I ever justified myself because I attend church, sing in the choir, and do service work? Do I judge others for their lack of participation or involvement?

_____

_____

_____

_____

3. After self-examination in Steps Four through Six, have I been struggling with self-hatred and shame?

_____

_____

_____

4. Do I realize that the "secret sins" of pride, judgment, and comparison are just as serious as the more blatant ones?

_____

_____

_____

_____

5. Have addiction and adversities humbled me enough to open the door to God's forgiveness?

_____

_____

_____

## Declared Not Guilty  *Romans 3:23-28*

1. Steps Six and Seven are one path to *acceptance* of this verse: all of us have fallen short, not only of our own ideals, but also of God's glory. Have I been trying to "measure up" and show God that I can "be good" by doing good works? How have I tried to show him that I am okay?

_____

_____

_____

_____

2. Can I now trust in faith that Jesus will not only make up for my weaknesses but will also begin to remove shortcomings as I surrender humbly to his will? If not, why?

_____

_____

_____

**Into the Open** *Philippians 2:5-9*

1. Have I disguised my addiction by covering it up with a good image? Have I hidden behind a good reputation?

_____

_____

_____

_____

2. Do I still fear that others will find out about my addiction? Will my pride be hurt if someone knows the extent of it? Am I willing to share if it will help others?

_____

_____

_____

_____

3. Can I release to God my self-centered fears of being known and of losing my image? If so, write a prayer to God expressing your desire to do so:

_____

_____

_____

**Eyes of Love** *1 John 5:11-15*

1. God already sees us as we will be when his work is done. Am I aware of any blocks that keep me from asking him into my heart to do that work? What are they?

_____

_____

2. Is my confidence in God's willingness to remove my shortcomings renewed? How and why?

_____

_____

_____

_____

_____

_____

_____

"Shortcomings" is a very polite way of saying *sin, weakness, defects in character, addiction, compulsion, dependency*—or a thousand other conditions and symptoms that indicate we are falling short of the glory of God and the lives he has called us to live. Asking God to remove our shortcomings is always a joint venture between us and him. Since we have spent much of our lives proving we can't fix ourselves, it is time to finally ask God to do what we will never have the power or insight to do ourselves.

### A Prayer for Step 7

*Dear God,*
*Search my heart and reveal to me any arrogance or pride that is separating me from you, the people around me, and the person you have called me to be. My shortcomings are numerous, and my attempts to fix them always end in failure. Please remove these shortcomings from me. Do for me what I cannot do for myself. Give me the courage to do whatever it takes to become victorious over these problems. Thank you for the work you are doing in me and for the opportunity to transform my life. Amen.*

## PROFILE

Stan was a middle-aged man who had been caught by his wife in a second affair. She wasn't sure that she would stay with him, and this propelled him to seek counseling and begin a recovery program. He came out of some denial that his behavior indicated a sexual addiction. He had been telling himself that he had a right to have these affairs, that they wouldn't hurt anyone. But in working Step Four, he had to inventory the morality of his choices and acts. In Step Five, he had to discover his part in the situation and face the exact nature of his wrongs. These character defects allowed Stan to delude himself into thinking that he could manage and control the effects on his marriage of sexually acting out. The first seven steps taught him that he couldn't.

To work Step Eight, Stan went back to his inventory to find the list of people he had harmed. His sponsor and counselor assisted him to see that he had harmed many more people than just his wife and the women with whom he had the affairs. By acting out sexually, he had stolen not only the trust of his wife and the other women's husbands, but also all of their emotional security and faith in the stability of their marriages. His choices also shaped his relationship with each of his children. He had less time for activities, was less available emotionally, and was unable to truly guide his children when he was actively deceiving their mother. The spiritual impact for the future was huge.

In recognizing the impact of his behavior on his family and those with whom he had been involved, Stan felt his conscience begin to stir. His heart became willing to make amends to all these people, even if this was frightening, because he wanted to be free of the shame of continuing such hurtful behavior.

## STEP **EIGHT**

### *We made a list of all persons we had harmed and became willing to make amends to them all.*

In our journey through the Twelve Steps, a spiritual awakening forms the purpose of healing our relationships with self, others, and God. To be free of addiction, we must be willing to go to any lengths to achieve this spiritual healing. Step Eight is crucial to living out this goal, even if we are threatened by the possibility of facing our most difficult relationships.

We have been in the midst of transforming our thinking, behaviors, and attitudes. Our pride and false self have been punctured to reveal the new "skin" of a humble, teachable spirit.

However, considering Step Eight may activate our egos and defensiveness once more. Just imagining having to make amends to some of the painful relationships of the past can activate fear of the possible humiliation in store when we contact these people. "It's in the past; it's over and done with; nothing can be changed now," we will want to protest. Of course, we also want to point out to our sponsors and trusted advisors that these are people who harmed *us.* "When do *they* have to make amends?" we cry. All these excuses are ways to resist forgiveness. We may fear that other people will perceive that we condone their behavior, or that we are allowing others to take advantage of us.

But, if we are to achieve lasting recovery from addictive substances and behaviors, forgiveness is required. Step Eight requires the shattering of our pride once again, to develop the deeper humility that opens the way to forgiveness. God expects us to extend mercy to other people, just as God has extended mercy to us. (See the parable of the unforgiving debtor in Matthew 18:23-35.) Unless we transcend our own hurts and have mercy on others who have harmed us, we will remain in the prison of our addictions. Lasting recovery and serenity will continue to elude us.

To make our list, we first have to identify and admit the harm we have caused others. Some of us may cling to the belief that our addiction didn't harm anyone but ourselves, either because no one knew about it, or because we drank only at home. There are many other excuses, but we are now going to be even more drastic in taking responsibility for ourselves because we want spiritual freedom. Although it is challenging, we must now examine our unintentional sins and how unaware we have been of the harm we have done to others. We have not allowed ourselves to be aware of the fact that alcohol (and other addictive substances and behaviors) affects our moods, emotions, and judgment. The harm may not be tangible, but it is damaging nonetheless. What about family members who suffered our silent scorn, pouting, or depressive bouts? What about the emotional effects of our angry tirades? What about subjecting our family to our poor judgment with money, time, decisions for work, and moving from city to city? Thinking along these lines, we can see that our list may be quite extensive.

This step is only for list making and for becoming willing to make amends. We must work with our sponsor to reach a decision about whom we will make direct amends to when we work the next step. If we put off making our list because we are thinking of Step Nine, then we are not fully engaged in the task of Step Eight.

Whether we have made poor choices under the influence or have just been insensitively unaware of our effect on others, in Step Eight we become willing to amend our ways and take responsibility for ourselves. We may put off working this step because we are afraid of the responses we will get. We are not responsible for how *they* respond, only for our *willingness* to set the relationship right.

Our resentment and defensiveness—natural responses to unhealthy relationships—will block us from offering forgiveness to the people on the list. We may have review Step Four for our part in these situations. The prophet Hosea, speaking for God, described the law of sowing and reaping: "Plant the good seeds of righteousness, and you will harvest a crop of love. Plow up the hard ground of your hearts, for now is the time to seek the LORD, that he may come and shower righteousness upon you" (Hosea 10:12). Steps Four through Nine are actually for "plowing up the hard ground of [our] hearts."

As we become clear about our responsibility for our crop of anger, grief, and sadness over broken and lost relationships, we can be more open to the process of making amends. The "plowing up" that occurs by taking these steps and seeking God's will is actually the beginning of a new crop of forgiveness and compassion toward those we have hurt and those who have hurt us. We may still have to face negative consequences from our addictive behaviors, but our heart work will become life-changing recovery. Realizing that our own wrongdoings have been forgiven and that we are on a path of new life, we are more apt to offer forgiveness and understanding to others. This act of humility and forgiveness opens us to the willingness to make amends.

One more thing: Often when we make a list of people we have hurt, we leave off the person who has experienced more pain than anyone else—*ourselves*. You must acknowledge that you have hurt yourself, and you must put your name at the top of the list of people you have harmed. Willingness to forgive ourselves and make amends to ourselves makes it easier to do the same for others.

We are ready for Step Nine.

# QUESTIONS FOR STEP **EIGHT**

**Making Restitution** *Exodus 22:10-15*

1. How have I failed to respect the property of others?

_____

_____

2. Have I been so harmed or condemned by others that I have avoided responsibility for myself? By whom and how?

_____

_____

_____

_____

3. What excuses have I used for not looking at my behaviors?

_____

_____

_____

**Unintentional Sins** *Leviticus 4:1-28*

1. In what areas have I unintentionally harmed others with my words, moods, self-pity, depression, anger, or fears?

_____

_____

_____

2. In what ways have I acted thoughtlessly without regard for others' needs or feelings? When? To whom?

_____

_____

### Scapegoats *Leviticus 16:20-22*

1. Have I been putting off making a list because I am afraid of some responses? Whose?

_____

_____

2. Have I held on to shame about a certain incident or relationship? What am I willing to do to let go so that I can become willing to make amends?

_____

_____

_____

3. Is there someone I am having trouble forgiving who blocks my willingness? Who?

_____

### Overcoming Loneliness *Ecclesiastes 4:9-12*

1. How have I allowed isolation due to shame and guilt to keep me from supportive relationships?

_____

_____

2. What is the role of shame and guilt in my isolation?

_____

_____

3. Am I willing to forgive myself for the hurt I have caused others? Write a prayer of willingness to forgive and ask for God's grace to heal these relationships.

_____

_____

_____

**Forgiven to Forgive** *Matthew 18:23-35*

1. Are there people on my list that I am having trouble forgiving for *their* part in our relationship? Who and why?

   _____

   _____

   _____

   _____

2. What keeps me from letting others off the hook? Fear? Resentment? Caretaking?

   _____

   _____

   _____

   _____

3. What blocks me from forgiving others for the wrongs done to me?

   a. Fear of what others would think of me? (Pride?)

   _____

   _____

   b. Fear of letting others see my hurts?

   _____

   _____

   c. Fear of conflict? Protecting others' feelings to avoid conflict?

   _____

   _____

   _____

**The Fruit of Forgiveness** *2 Corinthians 2:5-8*

1. Is there anyone on my list of whose behavior I do not approve? Who? Why?

_____

_____

_____

2. Am I willing to let go of judgment and disapproval to open myself to working this step?

_____

_____

3. Have I been so afraid of rejection that I have delayed willingness to make amends? Who could reject me and why?

_____

_____

_____

**Reaping Goodness** *Galatians 6:7-10*

1. What "crop" did I sow while practicing my addiction?

_____

_____

_____

2. Describe the correlation between healthy living and acceptance of the consequences for my addiction/behavior:

_____

_____

_____

STEP *9*

# PROFILE

Making direct amends must be done under the supervision of a sponsor/advisor. Not everyone on the list of harms will need direct contact. In Stan's case, making direct amends would be treacherous because of the potential to further destroy the marriages of those involved. To talk to the husbands or contact the women would be disastrous to the possibility of their moving past the harm already done. To avoid injuring these people on Stan's list, his sponsor and counselor agreed that his amends to these women and their husbands would be to have *no contact* by e-mail, phone, or in person. He would have to make *living* amends by learning to treat women as people, not as objects of his pleasure (present here are defects of ego, arrogance, and devaluing). This meant that he would have to change his behavior around all women as part of his recovery. It also meant that he would have to accept any consequences that came his way, if any of these women filed suit or if their husbands retaliated in some way.

The *direct amends* would be to Stan's wife and children, because they needed direct expression of his sorrow over his behavior for their own healing. Besides a direct verbal statement to his wife, he would also have to make living amends to her. He must learn to treat his wife with more respect, honor, and value, to let her know how important she is to him by his words and behaviors.

For his children, Stan would have to verbally admit his wrongs, depending on how much they knew about the affairs, and also to commit himself to model a healthy marriage in everyday life with their mother.

Step Nine sounds very exacting, but it is the beginning of a lifetime of changed behavior. Like Stan, we must be willing to continually amend our attitudes and actions with everyone. The verbal admission of guilt and request for forgiveness must be followed by a changed heart and changed treatment of those we have harmed.

## STEP **NINE**

*We made direct amends to such people wherever possible, except when to do so would injure them or others.*

In Step Nine, we put into practice the principles of the first eight steps: powerlessness, restoration to sanity, surrender, inventory of wrongs, willingness, and seeking help. To all this we add making amends.

The word *amend* means "to change." This is not an apology step of groveling self-humiliation. Instead, it is admitting to the people we have wronged that we know and understand the pain we have caused, and that we are committed to changing our behavior so that we will avoid causing any more pain. This step is about *direct* amends wherever possible, so we will go to these people personally or write them a letter. When we are face-to-face with these people, we need to have the previous steps' principles at work in us to be able to accomplish our goal.

Why would we put ourselves at such risk of exposure and shame? Step Nine offers us the opportunity to become free from the past. We can heal our relationships with others, with God, and with ourselves. In Genesis 33:1-11, we see this step in action as Jacob offered financial amends to his brother Esau by sending flocks of livestock before they met face-to-face. He was totally fearful of Esau's reaction to seeing him again after all the deception and thievery Jacob had practiced at Esau's expense. Jacob had to experience being deceived himself before he gained enough humility to recognize his faults.

The positive, healing outcome of this relationship was years in the making. In the same way, we have been through the pain of addiction, and now we are on a path of recovery that takes time. We must be willing to accept whatever response we are given. We must be willing to repair and resolve whatever has broken down in the relationship, even if the other rejects our offer to do so. As with Jacob, our willingness to go the extra mile is part of the spirit of Step Nine. The gifts Jacob sent to Esau were part of making restitution for the injury he had done and an expression of humility for his wrongs.

In Step Nine, we also become more realistic about ourselves and clean our side of the street, so to speak. When we are willing and open, God seems to give us a nudge to remind us of past promises on which we have not followed through. We may have damaged others' trust in us. We may have had extensive intentions, yet we can show no tangible evidence of those big plans and ideas. David had the experience of remembering an unfulfilled promise, as recorded in 2 Samuel 9:1-9. Like David, we need reminders of promises we have left unfulfilled. Step Nine gives us the assignment of remembering and acting on this.

*Making direct amends wherever possible* really challenges us to take opposite action from what our addictive personality would do automatically. Addictive behavior would be to cover up, hide, and avoid seeing anyone who might be angry with us or upset by our actions. Jesus challenges us in the Sermon on the Mount:

> *So if you are presenting a sacrifice at the altar in the Temple and you suddenly remember that someone has something against you, leave your sacrifice there at the altar. Go and be*

> *reconciled to that person. Then come and offer your sacrifice*
> *to God. When you are on the way to court with your adver-*
> *sary, settle your differences quickly. Otherwise, your accuser*
> *may hand you over to the judge, who will hand you over to*
> *an officer, and you will be thrown into prison.* (Matthew
> 5:23-25)

Jesus knew that if there is a broken relationship with resentment on one or both sides, we are not spiritually free to wor-
ship God. The harmed person could also put that resentment
into action and create great pain for us in retaliation. In other
words, spiritual and physical bondage are the consequences of
harming others with no attempt to repair it. When we learn to
set right, to the best of our ability, the situations in which we
have caused hurt, and actually change our behavior to stop the
harmful results, we are turning from the old addictive pattern
to new recovery behavior.

Step Nine places an astounding call on our lives to repair our
relationships, transform our inner self, and learn a new way of
living. In Ezekiel 33:10-16, there is a list of amending actions:
to return what was stolen, to obey God's life-giving laws, and
to stop doing what is evil. When we confront the utter self-
centeredness which has motivated the actions, drives, goals,
and feelings of our lives, we may be daunted by the enormity
of the recovery life. We may wonder whether this new life is
really possible for us. We may have observed people who have
attempted recovery from addiction, only to return to drinking,
overeating, and sexually acting out. We may wonder if continual recovery is possible.

Our response must be to allow God to do his work in us by
surrendering the outcomes and simply taking action. Recovery
is possible if we stay the course and take one day at a time.

Working the first eight steps creates a readiness and willingness to *assess* our past mistakes, even when this is uncomfortable. In Step Nine, we actually *take action to correct* them. In

Luke 19:1-9, Zaccheus came to Jesus and was inspired to take an inventory of himself. He recognized that he had harmed others as a part of being a tax collector for the Roman government. When he realized this, he publicly promised Jesus that he would amend his wrongs and make restitution for them. Jesus commended his attitude and actions as evidence of his spiritual change (i.e., salvation). This demonstrates the critical importance of Step Nine. We are in the process of spiritual development, and making amends is the first public display of our recovery from addiction and sin.

The amends process will often present situations that call for financial restitution. How will we respond? Zaccheus made amends by giving away half of his wealth. Then he gave more to people he had cheated, face-to-face. This is an example of direct amends.

The person who can make direct amends visibly shows humility, compassion, and the realization of his place before God. Salvation comes as we start to think more of others than of ourselves.

The amends process in Steps Eight and Nine brings out the "unfinished business" in our lives. We may discover past traumas that must be faced and dealt with if we are to maintain our recovery. We need to talk to our sponsor, counselor, or other trusted advisor so that we are not working with such issues alone, but they must be dealt with and resolved or they will follow us daily as though we were chained to them. We may not have caused or asked for these traumas to occur, but we may have to make amends to ourselves for playing the victim or curtailing our lives as a result of trauma. Step Nine allows us a new kind of freedom with ourselves, other people, and God.

Restoration of relationship with self is an important outcome of Step Nine. There is no more need to run when we have gone face-to-face with those we have harmed and sought to make things right with them. We no longer need to run because the slate is clean. We no longer need to speculate about forgiveness—we have forgiveness.

As we allow Step Nine to work in our lives, a new set of attitudes begins to emerge. Because of the life-changing relationship with God they developed, the first one hundred alcoholics to follow the Twelve Steps found that they could promise these results:

> We are going to know a new freedom and a new happiness. We will not regret the past nor wish to shut the door on it. We will comprehend the word serenity and will know peace. No matter how far down the scale we have gone, we will see how our experience can benefit others. That feeling of uselessness and self-pity will disappear. We will lose interest in selfish things and gain interest in our fellows. Self-seeking will slip away. Our whole attitude and outlook upon life will change. Fear of people and economic insecurity will leave us. We will intuitively know how to handle situations which used to baffle us. We will suddenly realize that God is doing for us what we could not do for ourselves. (Reprinted from *The Big Book*, pages 83-84, with permission of A.A. World Services, Inc.)

When we work the Twelve Steps to the best of our ability, they become realities in our hearts and lives. These are the changes we can expect when we earnestly seek the spiritual structure for life described in the Twelve Steps.

# QUESTIONS FOR STEP **NINE**

**Long-Awaited Healing** *Genesis 33:1-11*

1. Who are the people on my Step Eight list who strike the most intense fear in my heart when I think about making amends, face-to-face?

_____

_____

_____

2. Do I have supportive people to help me gain willingness to take such a challenging step? Do I have an advisor or sponsor to work with me?

_____

_____

_____

**Keeping Promises** *2 Samuel 9:1-9*

1. How have my thoughts, opinions, and ideas affected the decisions I have made?

_____

_____

_____

2. Is there anyone to whom I owe amends due to forgetting, either on purpose or unintentionally, to fulfill a promise?

_____

_____

_____

_____

**Covering the Past** *Ezekiel 33:10-16*

1. What forms of harm listed in Step Eight do I resist giving up in order to make amends with another?

_____

_____

_____

2. What fears keep me from the life-giving process of Step Nine?

_____

_____

**Making Peace** *Matthew 5:23-26*

1. What is my usual response or reaction to brokenness?

_____

_____

2. Does my amends list include people that have something against me? If so, do I have difficulty finding the courage to deal with them?

_____

_____

_____

**From Taker to Giver** *Luke 19:1-10*

1. List financial amends that you owe. Name the people and amounts:

_____

_____

_____

2. Am I willing to go to any lengths to offer amends? What risks are involved?

_____

_____


## Unfinished Business *Philemon 1:13-16*

1. How far will I go to restore a relationship with another person, with God, and with myself?

_____

_____

_____


2. Do I have any unfinished business left on my list? List these categories:

Money owed to people, jobs, businesses:

_____

_____

Any laws broken:

_____

_____

Broken, painful relationships:

_____

_____


3. Am I waiting for the certainty of forgiveness before I make amends? Am I willing to take the risk? Explain:

_____

_____

**A Servant's Heart** *1 Peter 2:18-25*

1. What am I afraid will happen when I attempt to make amends?

_____

_____

_____

2. Do I fear that painful consequences will cause me suffering if I make amends? If so, what is the worst that could happen?

_____

_____

_____

3. Do I trust God's will for me if I follow the challenge of Step Nine?

_____

_____

4. Which of the Twelve Steps do I need to focus on before I make these fearsome amends?

_____

_____

It's one thing to say you are sorry. It's another thing to prove it. Anyone can make a phone call and ask for forgiveness. At least they can enter the recovery process that results in confessing wrongs to another person and asking forgiveness. But it is the courageous person of character who wants to right the wrong, restore the loss, or pay back what was taken or owed in any way possible. Making amends is a powerful way of setting things straight, and it leaves others better equipped to do what you have asked: *forgive you*. There is a price to be paid for freedom and it is called *restitution*.

STEP **10**

## PROFILE

Eleanor and her teenage daughter Josie had yet another fight. Lately, it seemed that they were always arguing over behavior, grades, attitudes, or activities. This time, Eleanor had really lost her temper. She allowed the argument to escalate to the point that she screamed her frustration and sense of help-lessness at Josey, unable to set an appropriate limit. Tears and slamming doors expressed Josie's feelings, and Eleanor broke down sobbing and went for a walk.

As she walked, she remembered to take Step Ten and inven-tory herself on the spot. Where had she been selfish? Where had she been fearful? Was she jealous about something here? Had she been dishonest about something?

In running the argument through her mind, she began to recognize that she wanted to control her daughter's attitudes and behaviors because she was having trouble accepting her maturing and needing more space. She saw that she was fear-ful that if she did not address her daughter's disrespectful atti-tude, it would carry over into other areas. Besides, it hurt her feelings—or was it her ego/pride that was hurt? Was she angry at her daughter, or angry at herself for not setting limits earlier and more effectively?

When she returned after the walk, Eleanor wrote answers to all these questions as quickly as she could. She called a sup-portive friend who helped her to process her feelings and heard her admission of wrongs. They also discussed a way to take responsibility for her part with her daughter without shaming, blaming, and further damaging the relationship. She made a commitment to talk to Josie calmly about all this.

Peacefully admitting her part to her daughter was difficult, especially when she had been disrespectful, but Eleanor wanted the relationship with her daughter more than she wanted to be right and judge her. Eleanor decided to humble herself and forgive Josie for her hatefulness. As lovingly as she could, she explained that her control was fear of letting her go, of her growing up. She apologized for the cruel comments she had made and for judging her daughter so harshly. Josie was quiet at first and made little response, but over time she was able to be more real with her mother about her own feelings of confusion about their relationship and the difficulties she was facing at school and with friends. In the future Eleanor would have to commit to taking inventory in the moment in order to stay calm and deal with the real issues.

## STEP **TEN**

### *We continued to take personal inventory, and when we were wrong, promptly admitted it.*

Step Ten is the first of the "maintenance steps." We have faced our powerlessness and utter dependence upon God for our recovery and serenity. We have assessed our assets and liabilities for our usefulness to God and others. After clearing away the debris left by the effects of our addiction, we are ready to accept that the underlying principle of working these Twelve Steps is spiritual character building rather than comfort and convenience. We are coming to accept that our purpose here on earth is to do the will of God more and more completely, but we will not be able to grow spiritually in recovery without working this step *continuously.*

The concept of this step is similar to the rigorous exercise program that marathon runners use to prepare for their events. A marathon is a strenuous mental and physical challenge, and success requires focused, purposeful energy. Recovery is also a marathon, a strenuous challenge that requires similar purposeful, focused energy to achieve. We must take one day at a time with consistent discipline to assure continuous sobriety and serenity. Step Ten allows for planned, disciplined time to develop spiritual strength and agility.

For many of us, physical exercise is hard to do consistently. We may complain that it seems boring and tedious. To "continuously take personal inventory" may also seem tedious and needless, a real downer when we want to enjoy our recovery. These are defects of ego and pride that are part of our sinful nature. The disease of addiction can use them to keep us from long-term recovery.

By adopting this spiritual exercise, we practice regular ego/ pride deflation that allows humility to continue to develop in our souls. The rewards are often delayed, but we are laying the foundation for staying sober and clean under any circumstances. We need to search ourselves spiritually to identify addictive thinking and out-of-control emotions before they throw us off balance. If we assess our defects as they arise, we can correct them promptly and stay on the path of recovery.

The Tenth Step is also written to remind us that we are human beings and that we will frequently be wrong! The step does not say "if" but *"when"* we are wrong. This also levels our pride and helps to keep us emotionally right.

The word *promptly* is written in this step for the addictive self in us that recognizes wrongs and faults, but delays in letting anyone know because of pride or ego. If we promptly admit and correct ourselves, we prevent the diseased thinking from taking hold in our minds and hearts, and we stay close to God. In the book of James, healing is said to occur when we confess our sins to one another (see James 5:16).

We must never weary of taking Step Ten. Each day we can

do spot-check personal inventories and push toward spiritual growth. This diligence allows us to achieve continuous sobriety and serenity. When we suffer, we often grumble and complain, asking "why me?" We may resist having to take inventory of ourselves again, but admission of faults and willingness to correct our wrongs bring eternal rewards in the spiritual realm. In other words, the labor involved is worth the suffering and the ego-puncturing that result from working the Twelve Steps, especially Step Ten.

After achieving sobriety and being clean for a time, we may think that all of our other defects should be taken care of once and for all. This would mean that we have no sin and we are fooling ourselves! "Continuing to take inventory" and admitting our faults allow humility to grow in our character as God does the forgiving and cleansing and shows that his word has a place in our hearts. Where our addiction once made us oblivious to our wrongs/sins, our conscience is being restored. God's word lives in us and we recognize our need for him.

We may notice that the concepts and the work of the last six steps are actually rolled into this one step: inventory, confession, recognizing defects, faults, and sins, and making amends. This is our new blueprint for living—our path through the woods of life. The continual loop of self-examination and the development of humility propel us into greater serenity and deeper connection with God, self, and others.

# QUESTIONS FOR STEP **TEN**

**Personal Boundaries** *Genesis 31:45-55*

1. In order to restore trust in relationships, what particular weaknesses do I need to set boundaries around?

_____

_____

_____

2. Is there a trusted person to whom I can clearly define my commitments? Who? What commitments am I willing to make?

_____

_____

_____

**Repeated Forgiveness** *Romans 5:3-5*

1. Do certain behaviors and character defects that show up in my Step Ten inventory point to a pattern? Which ones? What is being revealed about me?

_____

_____

_____

_____

2. Am I having trouble admitting these promptly and forgiving myself?

_____

_____

_____

_____

3. Do I give myself grace? Why or why not?

_____

_____

_____


**Dealing with Anger** *Ephesians 4:26-27*

1. What is my first response when I am angry? Lashing out?
   Stuffing down? Avoidance and covering up?

_____

_____

_____

2. How was anger dealt with in my family? How did my mother
   deal with anger? My father? Which pattern do I follow?

_____

_____

_____

3. When I am angry, can I promptly admit it? Why or why not?

_____

_____

_____

4. Do I have support people who can help me learn to deal with
   anger more appropriately? Am I willing to ask for assistance with
   this issue?

_____

_____

_____

_____

**Spiritual Exercises** *1 Timothy 4:7-8*

1. As this continual inventory is important for spiritual fitness, where in my daily routine can I set aside time to make self-assessment part of every day?

_____

_____

2. Do I have any resistance to evaluating my defects daily? What are my objections? What do I fear?

_____

_____

_____

3. An example of a simple, daily, personal inventory:

Where have I been selfish, dishonest, fearful, inconsiderate, or proud?

_____

_____

_____

What have I done right today?

_____

_____

_____

What do I need God's help with tomorrow?

_____

_____

_____

What am I grateful for today?

_____

_____

_____

**Perseverance**  *2 Timothy 2:1-8*

1. How do I see my recovery as a war against addiction and as a fight for my soul?

_____

_____

_____

2. How do I see myself as an athlete training for the marathon journey of recovery and serenity?

_____

_____

_____

3. Am I working in every season and situation, planting seeds of recovery by applying the Twelve Steps to my life?

_____

_____

_____

4. Where do I lose heart in fighting, training, and working through the Twelve Steps?

_____

_____

_____

_____

## Looking in the Mirror *James 1:21-25*

1. Have I been quick to recognize but not to take action in a particular area of my life or defect of character? If so, I can take
action without self-criticism by going back through Steps Six
and Seven, then Eight and Nine on that particular area or
defect.

_____

_____

_____

_____

2. On what area or defect do I need to take action today? This
week? This month?

_____

_____

_____

_____

## Recurrent Sins *1 John 1:8-10*

1. Have I hoped for immediate release from my defects, as I may
have had from my addiction? Have I perhaps unknowingly
hoped that by doing all this step work I could attain perfection?
Write any thoughts and feelings that arise from reading this
meditation:

_____

_____

_____

_____

_____

2. Am I clear that I still need inventories to continue my spiritual growth? In other words, have I developed enough humility to accept that inventories will be a regular part of my journey? Explain:

_____

_____

_____

_____

3. Am I sensing that my conscience is returning or developing so that I more easily recognize my faults? Am I humble enough to admit them more readily? Record any progress you've noticed in your conscience:

_____

_____

_____

_____

Our lives require an ongoing evaluation of our thoughts, deeds, desires, and motives. As long as we live in the time between the Garden of Eden and heaven, we will always have times when we need to stop what we're doing and search our souls for areas that need additional attention. We also need to evaluate our relationships and interactions with others and admit to ourselves that we've been wrong. When we admit that we've been wrong to the person whom we have wronged, we initiate reconciliation and open the possibility of a deeper connection. Admission of a wrong is not evidence of a lack of recovery or a weak recovery. In fact, a humble heart and honest confession have always been the hallmarks of successful recovery. Our recovery is never stronger than when we are open, honest, and humble enough to admit we have made a mistake.

## PROFILE

As a seminary-trained minister and a Christian of more than twenty years, Alex thought, "I already know how to pray. This step will be easy." Then he read, "praying only for knowledge of his will for us and the power to carry that out." It became apparent to Alex that he had always prayed for God to carry out *his own* will, hardly ever asking for God's will only. This was a different way of approaching prayer, and his resistance sprang up. What about the verses that say "Pray without ceasing," "Make your requests known to God," "Knock and the door will be opened"? He was encouraged by his spiritual advisor to simply try this for a while and see what God would reveal to him. After all, had he committed himself to work the Twelve Steps to their completion because life was working for him? No, he had troubles with his coworkers, his rebellious son, and his wife's addiction. He agreed to try Step Eleven as it is written.

The first result he noticed was that he had to let go of his arrogance, which had motivated him to bombard God with demands for life to turn out the way he wanted. By adopting an attitude of humility, his heart let go of its demands and recognized that God is in control. When his will was out of the way, he was more open to hearing from God. In his prayer time, he kept a notebook and began writing down the thoughts and nudges that came to him. Over time, he saw that God was leading him to speak to the right person at the right time or to visit someone who needed God's encouragement. It was amazing to Alex that he could be so close to God's heart and carry out his will when he stopped demanding things.

Some days, he had to ask God for the strength to stay out of other compulsive, controlling behaviors. With practice, this spiritual discipline became a lifeline of recovery toward serving God.

## STEP **ELEVEN**

*We sought through prayer and meditation to improve our conscious contact with God, praying only for knowledge of his will for us and the power to carry that out.*

Step Eleven is the next maintenance step, in which we practice a new way of living. In the first three steps, we commit ourselves to turn away from addictive behaviors and thinking. Steps Four through Nine help us to clean out the past, and now we can focus on the present. Step Eleven gives us our spiritual marching orders as we seek through "prayer and meditation to improve our conscious contact with God."

We simplify our prayer life by praying "only for the knowledge of his will for us and the power to carry that out." King David's song of praise in 2 Samuel 22 shares with us the specifics of David's conscious contact with God. God in his many attributes is active on behalf of his people, even a single person such as David or ourselves.

What started in Step Three with surrendering our lives is now expanded in Step Eleven. We seek the will of God in our lives on a more earnest level. We also request the power that we need to carry that out, beginning with staying sober or clean from our addiction. Our substance, behavioral, or emotional addiction cannot satisfy our spiritual hunger—we have proven that. We must now find a connection to God that goes beyond mere belief—it must be a relationship.

Step Eleven guides us to seek God for who he is more than for what he can give us. We have experienced God's grace and mercy, which ignited our recovery. Without God's continuing to act in our lives, however, we are left with our own unsteady heart, mind, and behavior. For long-term recovery, we must have God's power and help.

Using prayer and meditation as tools, we actively and continually seek conscious contact with God. An example of this type of prayer and meditation is found in Psalm 27. It reveals how God works in our lives; how through praise and trust, we can live in serenity. When we grasp that God sees each person as important and valuable, we can trust that our well-being is in his care.

Because God cares about us and loves us in wondrous ways, Step Eleven builds the foundation of our present recovery on our relationship with God. In Psalm 65:1-4, David points us to joy in this relationship as we realize that we are welcome in God's presence. Working Step Eleven makes this a daily practice. Prayer and meditation are the vehicles for attaining conscious contact. Prayer is speaking directly to God and meditation is humbly and expectantly listening to him.

The Eleventh Step is focused on the present, which is different from the steps that deal with the past and with introspection. After all the inventories of our past in addiction, in which we realize that we have missed the mark on God's will, this step leads us to seek God's will for us today. We grow in humility as we ask for knowledge of his will and acknowledge that the power to carry it out also comes from God. As we exchange our old lives and objectives for his new ones every day, we are establishing a new pattern of living by faith. The former pattern meant keeping secrets that kept us sick, but Psalm 119 offers us the secret that strengthens and heals us, which is God's Word hidden in our hearts. The secrets of old behaviors in addiction will bring destruction and death, but when we hide God's Word in our hearts we gain the ability to avoid addiction and sin against God. This must be a daily activity because each new day is filled with possibilities and temptations. Today, we choose the path of Step Eleven in meditation and prayer to recover daily and deepen our relationship with God.

One huge challenge of Step Eleven for any addictive personality is learning to wait on God. Isaiah 40:31 says, "But those who trust in the Lord will find new strength. They will soar high on wings like eagles. They will run and not grow weary. They will walk and not faint." Impatience is a mark of any addictive personality, which lives for the immediate fix, high, or relief that comes from the substance-abuse or compulsive behavior. Now, we must learn to wait upon the Lord if we want to find new strength for recovery. We may even become impatient with our progress, but when we are in recovery for the long haul, Step Eleven directs us to depend more and more upon God. The result is the ability to turn less and less to addiction for relief, comfort, and joy.

Though Step Eleven presents a simple approach to prayer and meditation, it is often difficult. Sometimes we resist because we fear that his will may be contrary to our own. This is when we must reach again for the humility to align our will with God's will, knowing that his light will keep us from the darkness of addiction. This spiritual step expands our tolerance of his light and gives us a previously unknown measure of freedom.

# QUESTIONS FOR STEP **ELEVEN**

**A New Hiding Place** *2 Samuel 22:1-33*

1. How was addiction a hiding place from life for me? Compare this
   with having God as a hiding place.

   _____

   _____

   _____

   _____

2. Describe how I experience "conscious contact" with God:

   _____

   _____

   _____

   _____

**Thirst for God** *Psalm 27:1-6*

1. What do I most seek from God?

   _____

   _____

   _____

2. What is difficult about trusting God with my requests?

   _____

   _____

   _____

   _____

**Joy in God's Presence** *Psalm 65:1-4*

1. What keeps me from accepting God's forgiveness?

_____

_____

_____

_____

2. What scares me about the knowledge of God's will for me?

_____

_____

_____

_____

**Finding God** *Psalm 105:1-9*

1. Is my life changing daily? Am I noticing when I am resentful, selfish, dishonest, or afraid today? Identify ways that I am changing:

_____

_____

_____

_____

2. Am I aware of others' feelings, needs, and rights? What have I noticed today?

_____

_____

_____

_____

**Powerful Secrets** *Psalm 119:1-11*

1. What am I hiding in my heart—secrets of old behaviors and issues, or God's Word?

_____

_____

_____

2. List what I can thank God for today:

_____

_____

_____

**Patient Waiting** *Isaiah 40:28-31*

1. How does impatience show itself in my attitude and behaviors?

_____

_____

_____

2. Am I impatient about my progress in recovery? Do I expect myself to "get it" the first time? Do I expect perfection?

_____

_____

_____

3. Why is it hard to "trust in the Lord"?

_____

_____

_____

_____

**Friends of the Light** *John 3:18-21*

1. In what areas of my life am I still afraid to seek God's will?

_____

_____

_____

2. When I think that I am hearing God's will, whose power do I act on? Am I tempted to do God's will in my own power?

_____

_____

_____

God wants us in a vibrant, growing, and intimate relationship with him. In the first ten steps, we were working to strip away and throw off anything that stood in the way of our walking closer to the path God has chosen for us. Now we must stop walking long enough to allow God's presence so profoundly into our lives that we walk in his will and totally under his power.

### A Prayer for Step 11

*Dear God,*
*Thank you for showing me the path that leads to you. Thank you for being with me throughout this journey, and for being with me now. Allow me to experience you in new and intimate ways. As I meditate on your Word, expand its meaning and deepen my knowledge of who you are and what you want for my life. When I am afraid, give me courage. When I am weak, give me your strength. And when I am distracted, give me clarity of purpose and the desire to carry out your will. Amen.*

# PROFILE

Pauline was facing the fact that her marriage was over, and that divorce was inevitable. Her pain and depression were excruciating. To stay out of her addictive behaviors, she worked closely with her sponsor to apply all twelve steps as she navigated the process.

In Step One, she *admitted her powerlessness* over her husband's behaviors and choices, acknowledged that she could not change him, and accepted that when she tried to do so, her life and emotions became *unmanageable.*

In Step Two, Pauline *came to believe* that God could *restore her sanity* around her desires to control and change her husband and the inevitability of divorce. In Step Three, she *turned her will over* to God in this situation, as well as her husband, her life, and the effects of the divorce on their children, trusting that in his sovereignty, *God would care* for all of them.

For Step Four, her sponsor directed Pauline to write out her resentments about her husband and her own participation in the marital situations that led to divorce. She also wrote out her fears of leaving the marriage and of the effects on her children. In the process of writing this *inventory* assignment, Pauline was able to release the pent-up feelings, and they seemed more manageable. Together, they identified *the exact nature of her wrongs,* and the character defects that were causing her resentments and fears.

For Step Five, Pauline made an appointment with her sponsor to *share* her writings, feelings, and insights. Together, they identified *the exact nature of her wrongs* and the character defects that were the basis for her resentments and fears. She still had many feelings of grief and sadness over the circumstances to process and live out, but with new knowledge of her own part, she felt empowered to move forward in peace. She felt encouraged to change the things she could.

For Step Six, Pauline became *entirely ready* to have her defects of control, resentment, fear, and selfishness *removed,* as she recognized that they were keeping her from being emotionally free and spiritually available for service to God.

Step Seven was a prayerful step of asking God to remove these defects that kept her from doing God's will. She *humbly asked* to be free of resentment, fear, and selfishness around her relationship with her husband, even through the divorce process.

In Step Eight, Pauline had to see the effects of her own attitudes and behaviors on her marriage, and how she had *harmed* her husband with her attempts to control him through criticism, judgment, and nagging. This was difficult to look at when she was feeling like a victim and very hurt by the process of divorce, so it took time and prayer to *become willing to make amends* to him.

For Step Nine, *making amends* would mostly have to be living amends. Pauline had to stay out of her husband's life, avoid controlling him or judging his behavior (even from afar), and *change* her communications with him when discussing issues regarding the children.

Step Ten would be to *continue to inventory* her thought life and identify when she was slipping into self-pity, fear, judgment, and resentments. Pauline would *admit* these failings through journaling and sharing with her sponsor, and speak directly to the person harmed when necessary. This would be very important to keeping her emotional balance during the divorce process.

Staying in spiritual balance (Step Eleven, *seeking God through prayer and meditation for his will and the power to carry it out*) became a nonnegotiable time for her each day. She needed time to pray to be in God's will with no requests. Just resting in his presence was very healing for Pauline. She felt closer to God despite the emotional pain from the changes in her life.

As she worked all these steps in order, she was *awakened* to God's presence in all of life. She sensed his presence and will in everyday activities, and she was able to *live out the principles* of honesty, responsibility, and compassion. Pauline's objective was now to share this spiritual way of life with others, such as those she sponsored, coworkers, and church members. This reinforced the spiritual and emotional lessons she was learning. In *the sharing,* her gratitude for all that God was doing in her life increased even though she would never have chosen divorce as an option. By working these steps, Pauline discovered that she could experience the joy of living even in the midst of painful reality. This is recovery: living in reality.

## STEP **TWELVE**

*Having had a spiritual awakening as a result of these steps, we tried to carry this message to others and to practice these principles in all our affairs.*

There are three parts to Step Twelve: the affirmation of our spiritual awakening, carrying the message of that awakening, and practicing these principles in our entire life.

By working diligently on the first eleven steps, we have acquired a healthier view of ourselves, others, and God. This has enabled us to live free of the bondage of our addiction on a more consistent and contented basis. Even if we previously believed in God, we have achieved a greater level of surrender, humility, and serenity than we ever imagined. Allowing the Lord Jesus to free us from the burden and compulsion of addiction takes a measure of faith and humility that is challenging even to experienced Christians. The addiction has painfully exposed our

human limitations, frailties, and absolute inability to save ourselves. The addictive self has only one focus: the next drink, the
next fix, the next bite, the next hit. Recovery through the first
eleven steps teaches us to surrender that addictive will and bring
it into line with God's will, which yields freedom from captivity.

Now we embark on working the second part of Step Twelve:
*carrying the message.* After living in the spiritual poverty of
addiction, alcoholics and addicts of all types are able to live a
full life in relationship with God and others. This good news is
too wonderful to keep hidden. "No one lights a lamp and then
puts it under a basket. Instead, a lamp is placed on a stand,
where it gives light to everyone in the house," says Jesus in
Matthew 5:15. An amazing expansion of our maturity in recovery occurs as we share our experience, strength, and hope with
others. We keep it alive in us as we share compassionately with
fellow strugglers. It becomes our spiritual mission to share the
message of recovery and liberation with captive addicts.

Freed from the tyranny of addiction by working the Twelve
Steps, we have a new outlook on life and a deeper connection
with God's Spirit. Working Step Twelve means that we must be
ready to share with anyone at any moment about recovery from
addiction. This does two things for us. First, we must tell our
story to another person about what we were like in our addiction,
what happened to convince us to seek recovery, and what we
are like now that we are released from addiction by working the
Twelve Steps. By reminding ourselves of the path we have trav-
eled, we keep denial from creeping into our thoughts and leading us to relapse. Second, our humility and compassion develop
as we share. Admitting to another that we are recovering from
addiction takes humility and the courage to risk being rebuffed,
yet we know where the other is, emotionally and spiritually. Our
sharing can be of powerful help to others. Taking on this responsibility to carry the message brings a measure of maturity.

The third part of Step Twelve is *practicing these principles in all
our affairs.* Practicing these principles involves the continual

application of all twelve steps to our life circumstances. Let's review the principles we have been experiencing through working the Twelve Steps:

**Step One:** We must recognize our powerlessness and the unmanageability of our lives daily.

**Step Two:** God removes our insanity and restores wholeness.

**Step Three:** We surrender to God and let go of control.

**Steps Four and Five:** We make an honest inventory of ourselves (not others) and share our confession with another person.

**Steps Six and Seven:** In humility, we seek help from God to cleanse us and fill us with new strengths.

**Steps Eight and Nine:** We recognize the harm we've caused to others and take action to heal our damaged relationships.

**Step Ten:** We persevere in the training of the Twelve Steps in daily life.

**Step Eleven:** Consciousness of God's presence is with us always.

**Step Twelve:** We give away what we have gained in our journey through these steps and remain in recovery in every life encounter.

Remaining in recovery is similar to what Jesus said to his disciples in John 15:5: "Those who remain in me, and I in them, will produce much fruit. For apart from me you can do nothing." We cannot practice these principles of the Twelve Steps without being connected to him, so our priority is to apply these steps in any problem, event, situation, job, or relationship—in other words, through anything that life throws at us. When we connect to Jesus by deepening our conscious contact, he enables us to live more effectively, responsibly, and joyously.

As we maintain our sobriety and persist in recovery by working the Twelve Steps, we find benefits that were not obtainable before. In the midst of addictive behaviors and substances, our lives may have seemed to wander meaninglessly, but now they are filled with purpose and direction. We learn that we can be content with the conditions set before us. We learn that we can accept and handle tragedy and stress with serenity and courage. We learn to appropriately connect to our loved ones and seek to live well with everyone we encounter, meeting them with compassion, grace, and acceptance. We learn that our relationship with God is the key to all of these tremendous gifts of recovery, and that an "attitude of gratitude" is the salve for any irritability or other emotional disturbance. We begin to see that the basis of life is partnership with God and people.

Our shortsighted purposes for our lives begin to fade as we realize that with God's help, we can conquer our fatal addiction. The miracle of this partnership with God is so awe-inspiring that we are encouraged to continue recovery no matter how arduous it may be. We realize that material worldly success pales in comparison to living vitally and purposefully. The book titled *The Twelve Steps and Twelve Traditions* of Alcoholics Anonymous states, "True ambition is not what we thought it was. True ambition is the deep desire to live usefully and walk humbly under the grace of God."*

*The Twelve Steps and Twelve Traditions* (New York: Alcoholics Anonymous Publishing, 1986), 124–25.

# QUESTIONS FOR STEP **TWELVE**

**Our Mission** *Isaiah 61:1-3*

1. How have I passed through the pain and despair of enslavement to addiction and moved into healing and freedom?

_____

_____

2. Having had a "spiritual awakening" after being set free from my addiction, am I excited or hesitant to share my experience, strength, and hope with others who are struggling with addiction? Why?

_____

_____

_____

## Our Story *Mark 16:14-18*

Describe the story of your spiritual awakening and how the first eleven steps have brought spiritual principles, truths, and healing into your life. Describe what you were like, what happened, and what you are like now.

_____

_____

_____

_____

_____

## Sharing Together *John 15:5-15*

1. Am I connected to the vine? How do the Twelve Steps help me to "remain" in him?

_____

_____

2. Is my recovery attractive to other addictive/compulsive people because I am becoming more loving rather than condemning those who need my help?

_____

_____

3. What am I doing to reach out with Jesus' love?

_____

_____

### Listening First *Acts 8:26-40*

1. What is my attitude about sharing my story of recovery: Am I reluctant to tell my story, or am I the type that wants to share too much, too soon, with too many people?

_____

_____

2. From either extreme, am I willing to wait for God's timing for sharing recovery?

_____

_____

3. Do I see my story as valuable to God's plan? Describe how.

_____

_____

### Talking the Walk *1 Timothy 4:14-16*

1. Paul encourages Timothy to "throw yourself into your tasks so that everyone will see your progress." What changes in my life can others observe since I have been sober and working the Twelve Steps?

_____

_____

2. Paul wanted Timothy not only to teach others, but to be an example. When I share my story with others, am I preaching, or sharing my experience, strength, and hope?

_____

_____

3. Am I able to let the other person make his or her own decision by relinquishing control and letting God do his work?

_____

_____

_____

**Never Forget** *Titus 3:1-5*

What do I remember about my last drink or my last binge? Describe that time, including actions, feelings, behaviors, and thoughts that led up to it and followed it:

_____

_____

_____

**The Narrow Road** *1 Peter 4:1-4*

1. Peter pointed out: "You have had enough in the past of the evil things that godless people enjoy—their immorality and lust, their feasting and drunkenness and wild parties" (1 Peter 4:3). What was so painful about my addiction that I became willing to suffer for Christ (1 Peter 4:1-2) the pains of recovery?

_____

_____

2. Does the approval or judgment of others keep me from sharing recovery? Do I fear negative rumors?

_____

_____

3. How can I work the Twelve Steps on this fear?

_____

_____

_____

## CONCLUDING THOUGHTS

Our temptation now is to think that we have *finished* the Twelve Steps. The reality is that the steps are never really *done* because we never quit growing emotionally or spiritually. By practicing the Twelve Steps, we have a path for life and a connection with God that yields greater humility and reverence for his grace and power.

You never have to wonder how to carry this message of transformation to others. It happens when you integrate the Twelve Step principles into every area of your life. You don't have to loudly proclaim the message; your changed life speaks for itself. Attending weekly meetings and working the steps are only meaningful if they result in a remarkable life that is noticeably different than before—without the same destructive habits and patterns. The message is carried further and better by a kind tongue than by articulate lips. So carry the message of hope and transformation as you love others with all you have and all you are.

We conclude with this blessing and encouragement from Peter:

*May God give you more and more grace and peace as you grow in your knowledge of God and Jesus our Lord. By his divine power, God has given us everything we need for living a godly life. We have received all of this by coming to know him, the one who called us to himself by means of his marvelous glory and excellence. And because of his glory and excellence, he has given us great and precious promises. These are the promises that enable you to share his divine nature and escape the world's corruption caused by human desires. In view of all this, make every effort to respond to God's promises. Supplement your faith with a generous provision of moral excellence, and moral excellence with knowledge, and knowledge with self-control, and self-control with patient endurance, and patient endurance with godliness, and godliness with brotherly affection, and brotherly affection with love for everyone. (2 Peter 1:2-7)*

Prayer for Recovery *Let me focus my will today on my eagerness to do the will of God (through working the Twelve Steps) and not to "chase evil desires [addiction]."*

# SCRIPTURE INDEX

# Find Healing in God's Word Every Day.

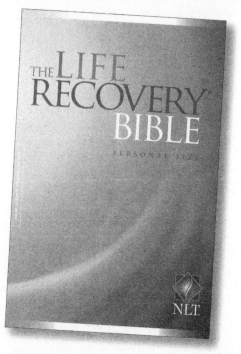

*The Life Recovery Bible* is today's best-selling Bible for people in recovery. In the accurate and easy-to-understand New Living Translation, *The Life Recovery Bible* leads people to the true source of healing—God himself. Special features created by two of today's leading recovery experts—David Stoop, Ph.D., and Stephen Arterburn, M.Ed.—include the following:

***Twelve Step Devotionals:*** A reading chain of Bible-based devotionals tied to the Twelve Steps of recovery.

***Serenity Prayer Devotionals:*** Based on the Serenity Prayer, these devotionals are placed next to the verses from which they are drawn.

***Recovery Principle Devotionals:*** Bible-based devotionals, arranged topically, are a guide to key recovery principles.

Find *The Life Recovery Bible* at your local Christian bookstore or wherever books are sold. Learn more at www.NewLivingTranslation.com.

Available editions:
Hardcover 978-1-4143-0962-0
Softcover 978-1-4143-0961-3
Bonded Burgundy 978-1-4143-0963-7
Personal Size Softcover 978-1-4143-1626-0

CP0107